CENTRAL AMERICA

BELIZE • COSTA RICA • EL SALVADOR
GUATEMALA • HONDURAS • NICARAGUA • PANAMA

Claude Hervé-Bazin

JPMGUIDES

Río Lagartos
Chiquilá
Progreso
Tizimín
Valladolid
Mérida
Chichén Itzá
Tulum
Golfo de México
Peto
Uxmál
Campeche
Península de Yucatán
Champotón
Becán
Chetumal
Ciudad del Carmen
Escárcega
Corozal
Amber
San Pe
Pico de Orizaba 5760 m
Gutiérrez Zamora
José Cardel
Veracruz
Alvarado
Catemaco
Coatzacoalcos
Bahía de Campeche
Frontera
Villahermosa
Laguna de Términos
Belize City
P.N. Tikal
Tumeff Islands
Oaxaca de Juárez
P.N. Benito Juárez
MEXICO
Minatitlán
Emiliano Zapata
San Ignacio
Dangriga
Monte Albán
Palomares
Istmo de Tehuantepec
Palenque
Maya Mountains
Placencia
Golfo de Honduras
Juchitán
Sra. M. de Chiapas
Ocosingo
Flores
Punta Gorda
Puerto
Sra. de Miahuatlán
Tuxtla Gutiérrez
Comitán de Domínguez
Puerto Barrios
Sa
*Corté
Salina Cruz
Arriaga
GUATEMALA
Santa Rosa de Copán
Puerto Angel
Pijijiapan
Vol. Tacaná 4093 m
Huehuetenango
Cobán
Vol. Tajumulco 4220 m
Copán
Tapachula
Chiquimula
Comayagua
Golfo de Tehuantepec
Quezaltenango
Mazatenango
Totonicapán
La Esperanza
Santa Ana
San Vicente
San Mig
Ciudad de Guatemala
Escuintla
Jutiapa
Golfo de Fonse
Sonsonate
Usulután
La Libertad
San Salvador
Chinande
Pacific Ocean
EL SALVADOR

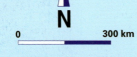

N
0   300 km

Central America

ancún

ozumel

Cayman Islands

JAMAICA

Kingston ⊡

Caribbean Sea

Cay

ELIZE

oatán
la
La Ceiba
Guanaja
Islas de la Bahía
Trujillo
Iriona
Puerto
Lempira
Mosquitia

edro Sula
geso
Juticalpa

DURAS
eque
gucigalpa
Danlí
Ocotal

Laguna de Caratasca

Puerto
Cabezas

Cord. Isabella

Costa de Mosquitos

Estelí
Choluteca
León
Viejo
Jinotega
Matagalpa
NICARAGUA

Boaco
ón
Lago de Managua
nagua
Juigalpa
Rama
Granada
Moyogalpa
Lago de Nicaragua
Isla de Ometepe
n Juan del Sur

Bluefields

El Castillo
Bahía Punta Gorda
Tortuguero

Liberia
Volcán Arenal
1633 m
Volcán Poás
2708 m
Puerto
Limón

Golfo de Papagayo
Puntarenas
Península de Nicoya
Alajuela
San José
Cartago
Puerto Viejo
de Talamanca

Montezuma Jacó
Quepos
Cahuita
Bocas
del Toro
Golfo de los Mosquitos

COSTA RICA
Palmar
Norte
Volcán
Barú
3475 m

La Concepción
David
Santiago

Península de Osa
Golfo de Chiriquí
Isla de Coiba

▲ Cerro Santiago
2826 m
Penonomé
Chitré

El Porvenir
San Miguelito
Colón
Cordillera de San Blas
Chepo
Canal de Panamá
PANAMÁ
✈ **Ciudad de Panamá**
Yaviza
La Palma

Archipiélago de las Perlas

P.N. de Darién

Golfo de Panamá

Península de Azuero

Reserva
Indígena

COLOMBIA

Pacific Ocean

Greenland

Canada

United States of
America

Atlantic Ocean

Mexico
Guatemala
El Salvador
Nicaragua
Costa Rica
Panama
Belize
Cuba
Jamaica
Honduras
Haiti
Dominican
Republic
Puerto
Rico
Venezuela
Colombia
Ecuador
Peru
Bolivia
Chile
Paraguay
Uruguay
Argentina
Brazil
Guyana
Surinam
French Guiana

Atlantic Ocean

N

0   4000 km

P.N. Int. La Amistad

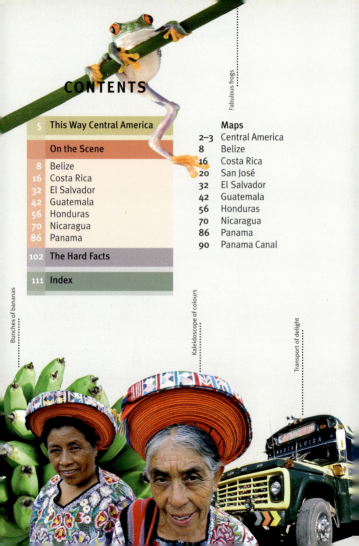

CONTENTS

Fabulous frogs

Bunches of bananas

Kaleidoscope of colours

Transport of delight

THIS WAY CENTRAL AMERICA

This was where the New World encountered Old Europe. Central America takes from the former the grandeur of the pre-Columbian civilizations and from the latter a social model imbued with pride and religious faith. Scattered across the territory, monumental Maya ruins emerge from the undergrowth of time and the jungle. Spanish colonial cities survive the countless earthquakes that have shaken the region.

Everything here imposes a crushing sense of history. On the margin of the new societies, the world of the American Indians—in Guatemala and elsewhere—fervently maintain their taste for colour, festivity and mysticism. The anger of the ancient gods keeps alive the flame of a string of volcanoes. Caribbean islands, tropical rainforest, national parks and varied wildlife increase Central America's attraction as a destination for eco-tourism.

Of vital strategic importance, the isthmus extends from Mexico to Columbia over about 2,000 km. Separating the Atlantic from the Pacific, it forms a land bridge between the north and south of the American continent. Its hypersensitive spinal chord, formed by the subduction of the Cocos tectonic plate, is made up of a hundred great volcanoes and about 150 smaller cones. The fertile soil in these exceptional natural sites makes them ideal land for cultivating coffee, one of the region main resources. But on the other side of the coin are the terrible earthquakes which from Guatemala to Costa Rica ravage the cities at irregular intervals. On both sides of the central mountain ranges hot and humid coastal plains stretch border the Atlantic and Pacific. It is there in the 20th century that the first so-called banana republics were born. Cut off from the outside world, certain marshy regions like the Mosquitia shared between Honduras and Nicaragua represent the last great virgin areas of Central America.

Nature's grandiose character here inspired in the pre-Columbian peoples their beliefs in the power of the elements. Covering more than 500,000 sq km, the Maya world embraces five countries on the isthmus: Mexico, Guatemala, Belize, Honduras and El Salvador. Buried deep within the tropical rainforest or simply timeworn, the mysterious ruins of the cities of one of the world's most brilliant civilizations are scatted over the four corners of this empire with uncharted frontiers. The Maya influence, diminishing the further one gets from the main centres, extended as far as Costa Rica. Beyond there, Panama already bore the mark of contacts with the peoples of the South American continent, including the Incas. The network of commercial and political relations among the pre-Columbian peoples extended over a vast territory: where the two civilizations met, Central America served as a bridge between its own culture and those of South America.

Reached by Christopher Columbus in 1502 on his fourth and last voyage, Central America represents the brutal start of the colonial era, when the adventurous and voracious Spaniards invaded to impose a culture and religion that made no concessions. The Conquistadors spread out from their main bases, reservoirs of seemingly inexhaustible riches: Mexico conquered by Cortés to the north and Panama by Balboa to the south. The lands in the middle were largely ignored as they seemed poor in resources. The American Indian peoples were subjected to a veritable genocide, exterminated by merciless wars or wiped out by new diseases.

From 1810, influenced by the liberal revolutions of the United States and France, the wealthy Creoles—born of Spanish stock on the American continent—began to stake a claim to the power denied them by Madrid. Dissent grew. They aspired not so much to justice as to power, to control a country they considered theirs. By 1821, all Central America was declared independent. With the exception of Panama, attached to Columbia, the territories united with Mexico. But from 1823, they split off again and created the Federal Republic of Central America. Slavery was abolished. Political instability was great; power struggles and internal tensions soon broke up the federation, with all the countries except El Salvador declaring independence in 1838 or the following year. Thereafter, each country fended for itself, liberals against conservatives, in unending fights that have in many places continued to the present.

In the course of time, Hispanic peoples intermarried with American Indians, giving rise to a range of societies unique in their kind, varying considerably in the proportions of American Indian and European cultures. Thus, Guatemala is still 40% American Indian, while Costa Rica is 85% of European stock. Between the two, El Salvador is almost entirely of mixed origin. In Guatemala, the Mam, Kichés and Cakchiquel to this day maintain their Mayan beliefs coloured by a touch of the Catholic cult of saints. In contrast in the towns, a new *mestizo* culture has grown up around the cement of of language and religion.

At the same time, people in a large part of Belize and practically the whole Caribbean coast of Central America are in their majority black. For the most part slaves exploited for their labour in the 19th century, their ancestors were sometimes brought in directly by the Hispanics—in particular in Panama—or they arrived, most of them, at a time when the Atlantic coast was in the hands of English pirates. Claiming to act in the name of the British crown, the buccaneers had made this region their private reserve, constantly harassing the towns and Spanish galleons. They imported slaves from Jamaica and the rest of the West Indies to work in the valuable hardwood industry. Inhabiting today Belize, Guatemala and Honduras, these Garífuna (known as "Black Carib" in the British colonies) are descendants of an Afro-Caribbean people whom the British forcibly exiled from the West Indies. They still speak an English patois dating back to the 18th century.

Intensive deforesting poses serious problems: the exploitation of the wood and slash-and-burn farming encourage erosion and destroy the soil's fertility. Luckily, in many of the countries, nature conservation has at last become a priority. Whether it be Costa Rica or Panama, over a quarter of their territory is protected through national parks or nature reserves. The other countries, eager to exploit the new wave of eco-tourism, are following suit.

The isthmus is home to more than half of all the world's known plant varieties. This is due in large part to the tropical climate and "terracing" of the vegetation zones, from sea-level up to the summits of the volcanoes, often rising to an altitude of 4,000 m (13,000 ft). From coastal mangrove, marshy savannah, jungle, rainforest or altitude forest up to alpine meadows, the bio-diversity is matchless. It offers opportunity to see the wildlife and perhaps even catch a glimpse in the undergrowth of the king of Central America: the jaguar.

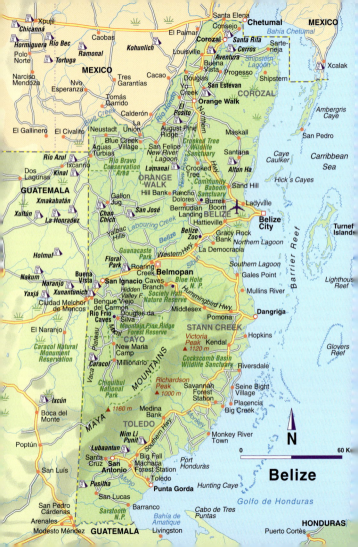

Belize

BELIZE

Belize has the ingredients of an all-round paradise. Its coral reef, in length second only to Australia's Great Barrier Reef, is a diver's delight, enclosing shimmering turquoise waters dotted with more than 175 tiny sand and coral isles known as cayes. Inland, two-thirds of the country is covered with thick forest, home to howler monkeys, armadillos, tapirs and jaguars. Beneath the forest floor lie buried the remains of undiscovered Maya sites, hidden for more than a thousand years.

At the base of the Yucatan peninsula, bordered by Mexico and Guatemala and fringed by the Caribbean, this pocket-sized country measures 280 km (174 miles) from top to bottom and 110 km (68 miles) across at the widest point. About a quarter of its 300,000 population lives in Belize City on the coast, and around 15,000 in the inland capital, Belmopan.

The official language of Belize is English—it was ruled by Great Britain for almost two centuries and was known as British Honduras until 1973. But the population is a very varied mix of Garífuna (African-Indian), Creole, Mestizo (Spanish-Indian), Maya, together with Chinese, Lebanese, Italians, and a community of German Mennonites. As a result, you'll hear a multitude of languages spoken in the streets of Belize City. Agriculture is the mainstay of the economy—citrus fruits, bananas and sugar cane—together with timber and, increasingly, tourism. Travelling inland can be something of an adventure, as the roads are usually unpaved, winding through jungle, swamps and savannah.

If you feel some affinity with the temperamental hero of *The Mosquito Coast*, you'll love Belize—the movie was filmed here. If you've ever fantasized about wandering untamed lands, exploring long-lost cities, lazing on empty beaches, swimming in pure lagoons, you may find that this is the place of your dreams.

A BRIEF HISTORY

3rd century BC
A pre-Maya community establishes a permanent settlement in Belize.

4th–9th centuries
The region is at the heart of the Maya empire, encompassing southeast Mexico, Yucatan, Guatemala, Belize, Honduras and El Salvador.

10th century
The great Maya cities are abandoned, ending an era of cultural and scientific development.

16th century
In 1502 Christopher Columbus encounters a canoe of Maya traders in the Gulf of Honduras. Hernán Cortés crosses southern Belize in the 1520s.

17th century
English pirates establish the first-recorded European settlement in 1638, later to become Belize City. Forestry is the major trade.

18th century
Black slaves are brought from Africa to cut the mahogany, used by the British furniture industry. More settlers come from Jamaica with their slaves and ultimately outnumber the Europeans. Spanish claims and raids are frequent. In 1798 the Baymen, as the settlers are called, win a decisive victory against the Spanish at St George's Caye.

19th century
Thousands of mestizos and Mexicans flock to northern Belize, driven out of their country by caste wars. In 1862 the territory is recognized as a British colony; this is much disputed by Spanish powers. Guatemala also claims sovereignty.

20th century–present
In 1961, Hurricane Hattie devastates Belize City. The official capital is moved 80 km (50 miles) inland to Belmopan. Belize City recovers and remains the social and commercial centre. Britain grants British Honduras total internal self-government in 1964. The country's name is changed to Belize in 1973; in 1981 complete independence is achieved, with Belize remaining a member of the British Commonwealth. Diplomatic relations are established with Guatemala in 1991 and an agreement reached under which Guatemala recognizes Belizean sovereignty in exchange for access to Belizean ports.

Sightseeing

Belize City

There's something distinctly Caribbean about Belize City, built on a peninsula divided by Haulover Creek, surrounded by mangrove swamp and criss-crossed by canals. Most of the houses are raised on stilts to protect them from flooding.

The two parts of town are linked by the manually operated **Swing Bridge**. On the North Front Street side of the bridge, the **Maritime Museum** documents the country's boat-building and fishing industry. The city's main shopping and commercial district lies at the southern end of the bridge. At the end of Albert Street, **St John's** is the oldest Anglican cathedral in Central America; it was built in 1812 from bricks brought as ballast on sailing ships. Nearby on Regent Street, the former governors' residence (1814), is now the **House of Culture**, a historical museum. If you walk back to the bridge by the Southern Foreshore, you will reach the **Bliss Institute**, a centre for the performing arts, then the **Supreme Court** (1926), overlooking Central Park.

The northern bank of the creek is mainly residential, with some attractive colonial houses. On Gabourel Lane, the former 19th-century prison has been restored and transformed into the **National Museum**, with a permanent display of Maya culture and changing temporary exhibitions. At the mouth of the river, the **Belize Tourism Village** has facilities for cruise passengers, including entertainment and access to tours.

At the tip of the peninsula, Fort George Point, the **Baron Bliss Lighthouse** looks over the harbour. This Portuguese noble of English origin visited Belize on his yacht in the 1920s and died on it, leaving millions of dollars to the city. He is buried in front of the lighthouse, which he designed and financed himself.

The Cayes

Boats and planes link Belize City with **Ambergris Caye**, the largest of these coral islands, 40 km (25 miles) long and less than 1 km (half a mile) wide. On the east side, not far offshore, is the barrier reef; the west coast is bordered by a lagoon. You can walk through the one small town, **San Pedro**, in about ten minutes. People come here for diving, from snorkelling to scuba, and the bountiful fishing. All the equipment can be rented on the spot. The southern part of the Caye is cordoned off as the Hol Chan Marine Reserve.

Closer to Belize City, **Caye Caulker** has around 1,000 permanent residents and is famed for its

lobster. Activities revolve around swimming, sunbathing on the beach called The Cut, and boat trips to the reef.

Half-Moon Caye is part of the Lighthouse Reef, the easternmost atoll, 112 km (70 miles) off the coast. In the middle of its exceptionally clear waters is the famous **Blue Hole**, a circular shaft reaching 125 m (400 ft) down to the sea floor, with several stalactite-filled caverns in its walls. The Half Moon Caye Natural Monument, in the southeastern part of the reef, is a national park devoted to the protection of the rare pink-footed booby that nests here.

Turneffe Islands, east of Belize City, are a maze of waterways and mangrove swamps, with good diving and fishing.

Excursions Inland

Altun Ha, some 50 km (30 miles) north of Belize City, is the biggest of the Maya cities discovered in Belize. It was an important trading centre, probably founded around the year 250. The name means "stone water". Temples, tombs and pyramids around two plazas have been unearthed and

The famous Blue Hole on Lighthouse Reef, originally a cave whose roof collapsed 10,000 years ago. | **Maya pyramid at Caracol** | **The clear blue waters around the cayes are irresistible.**

restored, and it's believed that many more buildings still lie concealed beneath the jungle floor. Archeologists discovered here a carved jade head of the sun god Kinich Ahau—the largest Maya jade sculpture in existence.

Lamanai (Submerged Crocodile) was inhabited from 1500 BC to the 19th century. The site can be reached during the dry season (October to May) by four-wheel drive vehicle, or by boat from Orange Walk, Guinea Grass or Shipyard. Don't stray from the track or you'll be trespassing.

Belize's northernmost city, Corozal, is built on the old Maya site of **Santa Rita**. Across the bay you can see the ruins of another site, Cerros.

The Western Highway from Belize City to Belmopan passes **Belize Zoo**, worth a visit for its outstanding feline collection. The nearby **Bermudian Landing Community Baboon Sanctuary** was created in 1985 to protect the fast-disappearing howler monkey. There's a small natural history museum in the reserve and a visitor's centre.

The most imposing building in **Belmopan** is the National Assembly on Independence Hill, decorated with a motif of Maya origin. See the priceless Maya artefacts in the Museum of Belize.

North of the city, where the Hummingbird Highway turns off the Western Highway, **Guanacaste Park** is home to rare animals such as the jaguarundi and the kinkajou. The park is named for the giant guanacaste tree, traditionally used for building dugout canoes.

Continuing along the Western Highway you'll pass the Mennonite community at Spanish Lookout, close to **San Ignacio**, the frontier town with Guatemala, and Santa Elena on the other side of the Macal River. The region is great for canoe trips. From San Ignacio you can arrange a tour of the **Panti Trail**, a botanical garden designed for the study of Belize's healing herbs in the ancient Maya tradition. A hand-pulled ferry takes you over the Mopan River to the ruins of **Xunantunich**, "Maiden of the Rocks". The main pyramid of this Maya ceremonial complex, El Castillo, is 38 m (127 ft) high, and there's a superb view from the summit. Near the top, an intricate stucco frieze illustrates the original appearance of the temple, and down in the temple forecourt, three stelae portray rulers from the Maya heyday of the 7th to 10th centuries. The famous Maya city of **Tikal** is a bumpy three-hour trip across the Guatemalan border. South of San Ignacio, **Caracol** (Snail) must have been one of the greatest Maya cities, though for many years archaeologists believed it to be nothing more than a small ceremonial centre. The discovery of an elaborately sculpted altar stone in 1986 revealed details of a Caracol victory over Tikal, once considered the most powerful of all Maya cities. The pyramid of Caracol 42 m (138 ft) is the highest man-made structure in Belize.

The road south from Belmopan, the Hummingbird Highway, meanders through the Maya Mountains to the port of Dangriga. Halfway between the two towns, **St Herman's Cave** shows signs of Maya presence. The nearby **Blue Hole** is part of the same network of caverns lacing the mountains, a point at which an underground river surfaces then disappears again after 30 m (100 ft), creating a turquoise-blue swimming pool. In the heart of **Mountain Pine Ridge** forest reserve, a 300-m (1000-ft) waterfall called Hidden Valley Falls makes a refreshing stop.

Just south of Dangriga, the **Cockscomb Basin Wildlife Sanctuary** is the world's first reserve devoted to the protection of the jaguar. Pumas and ocelots also prowl the dense forest, which is a paradise for birdwatchers as well.

At the tip of a sandy peninsula, separated from the mainland by a lagoon, **Placencia** is a tiny Garífuna village with the country's only real beach, 25 uninterrupted km (16 miles) of sand.

From Punta Gorda you can visit three Maya sites. At **Nim Li Punit** (Big Hat), a ceremonial centre discovered in 1976, 25 stelae were unearthed, including the largest sculpted stone found in Belize so far. **Lubaantun** (Fallen Stones) lies a 20-minute walk from the road; its pyramids and terraces are made up of huge blocks of stone that fit perfectly together. **Uxbenton** (Old House), overlooking the village of Santa Cruz, boasts 20 stelae, of which seven are sculpted.

Dining Out

Rice and beans form the basis of the Belizean diet, along with plentiful chicken and seafood, including lobster. The country has an enterprising cottage industry of snack bakers, especially on the cayes—just knock on the door wherever there's a sign for homemade lobster pie, fresh fruit juices, and so on. Rum is the favourite drink.

Shopping

In the crafts centre of Belize City you'll find objects from all over the country, such as woodcarvings and wickerwork. Black coral jewellery is on offer but be aware that it cannot be imported into other countries as it is an endangered species.

PRACTICAL INFORMATION

Banks. Opening hours vary from branch to branch, but as a general rule, Monday to Thursday 8 a.m.–1 p.m., Friday 8 a.m.–to 4.30 p.m. The Belize Bank accepts the major international credit cards; the other banks generally accept only local cards. Some banks charge a service fee for cashing travellers cheques.

Business hours. Monday to Friday 8 a.m.–noon and 1–5 p.m. Some businesses open on Saturdays.

Climate. Sub-tropical. In summer the temperature generally stays below 35°C (95°F). The rainy season lasts from June to August, and the hurricane season from June to November.

Currency. The Belizean dollar (BZ$), divided into 100 cents, is pegged to the US$ at a rate of 2:1. Coins from 1 cent to $1, banknotes from $2 to $100. Most hotels and restaurants accept American dollars, travellers cheques and credit cards. Many establishments will add a 5% service charge if you pay by credit card.

Health. This is the Mosquito Coast. Take insect repellent. If you intend to travel inland, you are advised to take precautions against malaria: consult your doctor well before your trip.

Language. English is the official language; Spanish is also widely spoken.

Security. Take care with your valuables, and avoid unfamiliar neighbourhoods after dark. If you rent a private boat to one of the cayes, don't pay until you reach your destination.

Shops. Open Monday to Saturday 8 a.m.–noon, 1–4.30 p.m. and 7–9 p.m.

Telephone. Roaming agreements exist with most international mobile phone companies. There is an e-mail centre in the BTL office in central Belize City, and Internet cafés in most towns and tourist centres.

Time difference. Year-round, the time is fixed at GMT –6.

Tipping. A service charge of 15 per cent is sometimes added to the bill in restaurants. Otherwise tipping is at your discretion.

Water. Make sure that all the water you drink is bottled.

COSTA RICA

Costa Rica—"rich coast"—is the name Christopher Columbus gave this country on his fourth and last voyage to the New World in 1502. The origin of the term is uncertain. He was probably hoping he would find gold here, or else he thought the country must be rich because of all the gold jewellery the native chiefs were wearing. Perhaps the country owed its name just to the country's lush and fertile landscape.

With an area of about 51,000 sq km (19,650 sq miles), Costa Rica is the third-smallest of the seven Central American countries. Between the Caribbean and Pacific coasts, the numerous mountain ranges have several volcanoes, some still active. The Meseta Central, the high plateau amidst the mountains, is blessed with a temperate climate and a fertile volcanic soil ideal for growing coffee. Three-quarters of the estimated population of over 4 million live up here, 85% of them of European origin. At the heart of the plateau, the capital San José is a modern city with lots of parkland and a high standard of living.

Costa Rica is a haven of peace on the Central American map. Since 1949, it has had a well-functioning democracy, an exemplary health service and efficient school system, thanks to which it can claim Central America's highest literacy rate. Up to now it is the only country in the world to have done away with its army. In 1987, its president Oscar Arias Sánchez won the Nobel Peace Prize.

Costa Rica's natural splendours provide its greatest riches. Its landscapes with their teeming animal and plant life scattered across rainforest, volcanoes and beaches, are protected by numerous national parks and nature reserves—particularly impressive since one of the world's highest rates of clear-fell logging still prevailed here in the 1980s. Costa Rica is putting all its cards on eco-tourism, that is, for visitors interested in nature and a unique travel experience off the beaten tourist track.

A BRIEF HISTORY

Pre-Colombian era

Costa Rica is settled by hunting and farming tribes of what came to be called Indians, migrating from the Amazon region or driven here by the Mayas.

16th–18th centuries

During a violent storm on his last voyage in 1502, Columbus seeks refuge in the bay of Puerto Limón. At this time, Costa Rica's native population numbers 300,000–500,000. Spanish conquerors looking for gold are scared off by impenetrable jungle and native attacks. and end up finding neither gold nor silver. Nonetheless, the native population is almost completed exterminated over the next 60 years. In 1563, the first Spanish settlers occupy the central high plateau. They found the town of Cartago and farm the fertile soil, living for 200 years cut off from Spain and from the colonial headquarters in Guatemala.

19th century

In 1821, Spain grants independence to its Central American colonies. San José is made the national capital. Slavery is abolished. From the date of its independence until 1838, Costa Rica is a member of the Central American Federation. After the latter's collapse, Costa Rica proves itself to be a much more stable country than its neighbours. This is due to the fact that from the outset, Costa Rica encourages literacy and prospers economically thanks to the import in 1808 of coffee plants from Cuba, making it the first country in continental America to create coffee plantations. At the end of the 19th century, banana plantations spring up along the Pacific coast, soon made accessible by a railway line to Puerto Limón. In 1889, the first free elections are held.

20th century–present

In 1948, civil war breaks out over a disputed election. Victor is the Socialist, José María Figueres. During his transitional government he nationalizes the banks, dissolves the Communist Party and the army and then transfers government to President Otilio Ulate, who was legally elected before the war. In 1987, President Oscar Arias Sánchez is awarded the Nobel Peace Prize for his peace efforts in Central America. For decades, the presidency has regularly changed hands every four years between the Christian Social Unity Party and the (conservative) National Freedom Party.

Sightseeing

San José

The economic and cultural centre of Costa Rica was founded in 1737 at the heart of the central valley and at the foot of some of the country's principal volcanoes. It became the capital 100 years later when the nation achieved independence. However, it did not really begin to prosper until the end of the 19th century, when the profits from its coffee exports began rolling in. San José was the third city in the world to introduce electric lighting.

The town has a lot of traffic, but it remains clean and efficient and enjoys a spring-like climate throughout the year. San José's frequent earthquakes have left few historical monuments, but the museums alone make it well worth a visit.

The layout of roads in the city centre is very easy to master: *avenidas* (avenues) run east-west, *calles* north-south. North of Avenida Central, the main business street, each parallel *avenida* has an odd number (Avenida 1, 3, 5, etc.) while each *avenida* to the south has an even number (Avenida 2, 4, 6, etc.); similarly, each *calle* east of Calle Central has an odd number, while each *calle* to the west has an even number.

The neoclassical **Catedral Metropolitana** towers over the **Parque Central**, not far from the intersection of Avenida Central and Calle Central. Just northwest of there, between Avenida 1 and Calle Central is the city's great market, the bustling and colourful **Mercado Central**. Besides the fruit and vegetables are stalls selling all kinds of craftwork, including leatherware and ceramics.

However, the real city centre is the **Plaza de la Cultura**, a little to the east. The tourist office is here, providing up-to-date information and street maps. On this square you'll also find San José's most important building, the splendid **Teatro Nacional**, inaugurated in 1897. It was financed with coffee export duties and is still regarded as Latin America's finest opera house. Costa Rican and Italian artists created the sculptures and ceiling paintings. The marble was brought from Carrara, the mirrors from Venice, and no expense was spared for the décor's exotic wood-panelling, gold, bronze, satin and velvet. Even if you can't go to an opera, ballet or theatre performance, do take a daytime look at the interior.

The **Museo del Oro Precolombino** displays its precious collections in the national bank's safety vaults beneath the Plaza de la Cultura. Particularly admirable is the meticulously crafted gold jewellery. The works of art assembled here demonstrate the

masterly metal-casting techniques of the country's early inhabitants.

San José is an ideal town for just hanging out. Sit on a bench and watch the busy comings and goings of the *Ticos*, as the Costaricans call themselves: street vendors of fruit or lottery tickets, shoe-shine men, schoolchildren and office-workers, sundry passers-by, everybody enjoying their town as much as you will.

The biggest park in the city-centre is the **Parque Morazán**. Its music pavillion, Templo de la Musica, stages regular symphony orchestra or brass band concerts. Bordering it to the east is the **Parque España** with the grand **Casa Amarilla** (foreign ministry) on the north side. In stark stylistic contrast is the pioneering Art Nouveau architecture of the **Edificio Metálico**. Its braces and beams were designed in France, manufactured in Belgium and assembled in San José in 1890.

One of the outstanding attractions of the city is the **Museo de Jade** on the 11th floor of the National Insurance Building. You can admire here the largest collection of jade in the Americas. Some of the rooms exhibit artefacts and jewellery fashioned by the pre-Columbian peoples who originally inhabited the region of Costa Rica. Particularly noteworthy are the *metates*, beautifully carved three- or four-legged tables used for grinding grain. The exhibits benefit from state-of-the-art lighting techniques, with many of the objects illuminated from the rear to bring out jade's magical translucency. Take time out on the museum's terrace to enjoy a splendid view over the town and the surrounding countryside.

East of the city centre, behind the old National Distillery (open to the public), is the **Parque Nacional**, bordered on the north by the National Library and on the south by the Asamblea Legislativa (Parliament). In the park, a fine bronze sculpture commemorates the victory of the Central American republics over the US mercenary commander William Walker in 1857.

A short walk from here, the **Museo Nacional** is housed in Fort Bellavista, headquarters of the national army until its abolition in 1949 (traces of bullet-holes still scar the tower walls from the revolution a year earlier). Its charming architecture includes a pleasant tree-shaded inner patio. The collections include impressive pre-Columbian gold and jade artwork, colonial furniture and various exhibits tracing the nation's including a special section devoted to President Arias Sánchez and his Nobel Peace Prize awarded in 1987.

Painted wooden carts were used to transport sugar cane, tobacco and coffee.

Claude Hervé-Bazin

Meseta Central

Explore the country's central high plateau, using San José as a base for day trips or longer excursions.

Looming north of the capital in the Cordillera de Guanacaste are some of the country's best-known volcanoes: the Poás, 2,708 m (8,885 ft) with one of the world's largest craters, the Irazú, 3,432 m (11,260 ft) and the characteristically cone-shaped Turrialba, 3,328 m (10,919 ft). Two excursions over the Meseta Central are described below, one through the northwestern and one through the eastern region.

Founded in 1706, the town of **Heredia** lies 10 km (6 miles) northwest of San José. Even today, the town's atmosphere still evokes its long colonial tradition in its beautiful parks and immaculate white-washed houses. The massive Church of Inmacula Concepción was erected in 1797. North of town, vast coffee plantations stretch to the horizon. Towards the end of the dry season, the coffee bushes are covered with white fragrant blossom. Each red fruit, harvested from October to January, contains two coffee beans.

Close to the international airport, **Alajuela** is the country's second-largest city and birthplace of Costa Rica's national hero Juan Santamaría. In 1855, the American mercenary commander William Walker had found refuge in Fort Rivas in Nicaragua, with Costarican troops in hot pursuit after he had tried to invade their country. Juan Santamaría, a young drummer-boy, sacrificed his life to set fire to the fort and force Walker to flee. Every year the anniversary of the hero's death is commemorated. His monument stands on Calle 2, northwest of the Parque Central. The full story is related in graphic detail in the nearby Museo Histórico Juan Santamaría.

About 15 km (9 miles) to the southwest is **La Guácima butterfly farm**, the oldest and biggest in Latin America. Guided tours take visitors through tropical gardens in which over 60 varieties of butterfly may be seen fluttering around. The farm breeds caterpillars and butterfly pupae for export.

Northwest of Alajuela is one of the most important coffee-growing regions of the Meseta Central. A narrow road leads through beautiful countryside to **Sarchí**, Costa Rica's most important craftwork town. The famous brightly painted ox-carts with the big wheels are made here—albeit less for their use than for their folklore interest. Several workshops are open to the public. The bright pink colour of the parish church makes an enchanting effect at sunset.

North of Sarchí, you will soon spot the silhouette of the still active **Poás**, Costa Rica's most "popular" volcano. It is possible to drive almost all the way to the summit. Its crater measuring 1.5 km (almost a mile) in diameter counts among the biggest in the world. In earlier times, its upper shell concealed a crater lake that gave off steam and the stink of sulphur. Since 1954, date of the last really big eruption, the volcano has kept more or less quiet, but a geyser that keeps on shooting up into the air, often several hundred metres high, is a clear sign that the Poás had not gone to sleep for good.

From the information centre, a footpath leads through the woods to the lovely **Laguna Botos**, 150 m (490 ft) higher up, a smaller old volcano last active several thousand years ago. As the first clouds begin to gather at about 10 a.m., you should make an early start to be able to enjoy the excursion under the best conditions.

Along the La Paz river, the **La Paz Waterfall Gardens** include a big butterfly house, a hummingbird garden, and footpaths through the rainforest along the water's edge.

East of the Barva and Poás volcanoes lies the **Braulio Carillo National Park**. Covering an area of over 47,700 ha, it is the biggest park on the Meseta Central. The park was created in 1978 as a protective area for the dense rain-forest through which an important expressway was built from San José to the Caribbean coast. In this way a refuge was preserved for several animal species. Thanks to the various levels of vegetation between the Caribbean coastal plain at an altitude of 50 m (164 ft) up to the 2,906-m (9,535-ft) **Barva volcano**, the forest reveals a multiplicity of ecosystems. All five big wildcats of the American tropics have their home here the puma, jaguar, ocelot, jaguarundi (or otter-cat) and long-tailed spotted margay. In all, the park has 135 species of mammal, among them 73 different kinds of bat, as well as 500 species of bird, including the sacred quetzal, the magnificent green and red long-tailed bird worshipped by the Mayas and Aztecs.

You reach the volcano summit either from Barva, a pretty little colonial village in the midst of coffee plantations or else from the villages of San José de la Montaña or Sacramento.

Continue on the expressway in the direction of the sea as far as the Río Sucio Bridge; 5 km (3 miles) further on, you can take the **Teleférico del Bosque Lluvioso** (Rain-Forest Cable Car) across the Bosque Lluvioso Nature Reserve and from a height of 35 m (115 ft) catch a bird's-eye view of the lush flora and teeming fauna. For 90 minutes you glide silently along a stretch of the jungle's treetops.

At the northern end of the Braulio Carillo, about 17 km (11 miles) southwest of Las Horquetas, you can visit the private **Rara Avis** nature reserve, a typical example of Costarican ecotourism. Zoologists and botanists accompany through the tropical forest. Don't forget, on all these reserves, that you're going through a wilderness and the paths are mostly muddy.

At the foot of the Irazú volcano 22 km (14 miles) east of San José, stands the town of **Cartago**, formerly the national capital founded by the conquistador Juan Vásquez de Coronado in 1563. The town has suffered so many earthquakes that the people did not bother to rebuild once massive church of La Parroquía on the Plaza Central. East of the ruin, the Basilica Nuestra Señora de los Angeles counts among the great Catholic churches of pilgrimage to the Virgin Mary. It houses the country's patron saint, the Negrita, a black Madonna with miraculous powers. Every year on the saint's day, August 2, thousands of pilgrims walk in procession from San José.

From Cartago, a winding road leads to the crater edge of the **Irazú volcano**, one of the country's main tourist attractions in the middle of rainforest. Just beneath the summit, you stumble on a lunar landscape of boulders and ashes. The volcano last erupted in May 1963, covering a large part of the valley with ashes—some of which blew all the way to San José. In the hollow of the crater is a small greenish-blue lake. On clear days, the view from the summit extends both to the Atlantic and to the Pacific.

Just 4 km (2.5 miles) east of Cartago on the road to Paraíso is the **Jardín Lankester**, known for its many varieties of orchids. The other side of Paraíso, on the banks of Cachí, an artificial lake popular with fishermen, is the secluded village of **Ujarrás** with its imposing ruined church. Southwest of the lake, in the village of **Orosí**, the Franciscan mission boasts Costa Rica's oldest church (1743) to have survived intact. Coffee plantations spread all around the village.

Turrialba, at the foot of the Turrialba volcano (3,328 m, 10,919 ft), is the seat of CATIE, the centre for tropical agronomy research and training, with a pleasant botanical garden open to the public. The town is a popular base for whitewater rafting expeditions.

Nearly 20 km (12 miles) to the north, in the village of **Guayabo**, is the country's most important pre-Columbian excavation site. An aqueduct, sewerage system and tombs are all that remain of a settlement abandoned some time after 1400.

Northwest Costa Rica

The country's most active volcano, the **Arenal**, 1,633 m (5,358 ft), in the southeast of the Cordillera de Tilarán, made its first appearance just 4,000 years ago. Since its eruption in 1968, when 80 people were killed and two villages destroyed, it regularly spews out lava or rocks and thunders non-stop. From **Lake Arenal** at night, glowing lava can be seen flowing down the slopes. The pretty artificial lake offers ideal conditions for wind-surfing. A road running around it takes you to Tilarán. From here, an unpaved track for off-road vehicles leads to the village of **Monteverde**, founded by American Quakers in 1952. A short distance to the east is the Monteverde forest reserve. One of the most popular of its trails is the Sendero Bosque Nuboso, which has boards along the way providing detailed information about the ecosystem. The paths are muddy, the forest is damp and you'll need rainwear. One of the guides can point out some of the 400 species of birds, among them perhaps the beautiful quetzal. At the park entrance, a Hummingbird Gallery attracts dozens of the forest's seven

Claude Hervé-Bazin

Turtles

Every year the female turtles come to lay hundreds of eggs in the warm sand of the beaches where they themselves were hatched. Then they cover them up and go back into the water. After about 50 days the babies hatch out. They have to run as fast as they can to the sea, to escape the claws of birds of prey. They are not yet safe when they reach the water, where voracious fish are lying in wait. The turtles and their eggs also face the dangers of human hunters. Costa Rica's government has managed, through state-organized collection of eggs, to ensure the native population a traditional source of income while still protecting the turtles.

species. Visits to the reserve should be arranged the previous day as the park allows a daily maximum of 120 to 150 people.

In the far northwest of the country is **Liberia**, capital of Guanacaste province and the centre of Costa Rica's cattle-breeding. The local national park surrounding **Rincón de la Vieja volcano** comprises waterfalls, fumaroles and bubbling mudpools.

Easily accessible from the Panamericana Highway, **Santa Rosa National Park** sprawls across the Santa Elena peninsula on the Gulf of Papagayo, open to the Pacific. Abundant wildlife inhabits the dry and airy tropical forest.

At **Nancite**, thousands of turtles come crawling up the sandy beach to lay their eggs in September and October.

Pacific Coast

The country's northwest is dominated by the **Nicoya peninsula**, 130 km (80 miles) long, whose white sandy beaches are still nearly all peaceful and unspoiled. On the north corner of the peninsula, the beach of **El Coco** is set in a pretty bay, but it can also get crowded. Just to the north, the **Playa Hermosa** is one of the country's most luxurious beach resorts. Also very beautiful is the sandy beach of **Tamarindo**, popular with surfers. Enormous leatherback turtles can be seen near **Playa Grande**. From

July to November (and specially in September and October), the **Ostional nature reserve**, further south, is invaded by hundreds of olive-green turtles who come to lay their eggs in the warm sand. Beyond the reserve, **Playa Sámara** is one of the country's most popular beach resorts, with a stretch of white sand. At the southern tip of the peninsula are the unspoiled sands of the **Cabo Blanco nature reserve**, a haven for monkeys and several species of sea birds, with 1300 ha of land and 1700 of marine area. At Playa Tambor, boat cruises are available for the **Isla Tortuga**. The island's waters are warm and its idyllic beaches framed by coconut palms.

In the upper parts of the Golfo de Nicoya on the north bank of the Río Tempisque, **Palo Verde National Park** covers a typical area of wetlands. There is a wide variety of ecosystems in a narrow space: swamps, salt- and freshwater lagoons, pasture, savanna and evergreen forests. The park attracts vast numbers of waterfowl of all kinds.

South along the mainland coast, **Puntarenas** was Costa Rica's biggest port in the 19th century, departure point for coffee exports. Today it has lost its importance, giving way to Puerto Caldera, port of call for most cruise ships. Further south, **Río Grande de Tárcoles** is home to crocodiles,

The spectacular cloud forest of the Monteverde Reserve in the Northwest.

Claude Hervé-Bazin

some of them measuring up to 4 m (13 ft) in length. Take a boat cruise for a close-up view of these dangerous beasts.

The sleepy little town of Quepos is the gateway to **Manuel Antonio National Park**. With its luxuriant tropical vegetation, this park is the country's smallest but also the most popular. Footpaths lead through the forest to the wonderful beaches of Espadilla Sur and Playa Manuel Antonio and further east to the bay of Puerto Escondido.

Near the frontier with Panama, at the southwesternmost point of the country, the great **Osa peninsula** juts out into the Pacific. The great **Corcovado National Park** is beginning to attract visitors to its richly diverse vegetation and wildlife. Thanks to its high annual rainfall, it numbers about 500 different varieties of trees.

On the other side of the Golfo Duce is the former banana port of **Golfito**. Since 1990, the government has set up a free trade zone here to boost the economy. Take a side-trip to the beaches of **Zancudo**, 15 km (9 miles) south of Golfito, and **Pavones**.

Limón

The Caribbean coast differs sharply from the country's other regions. Tropical humidity leaves it sparsely inhabited and regarded as Costa Rica's backyard. The largely black local population is English-speaking in contrast to the Hispanic, white inhabitants of the Meseta Central. Close to the Panama border, natives maintain their ancient traditions. Fine beaches and nature reserves are attracting more and more tourists.

Puerto Limón is hot and humid; the chief activity is loading bananas. Most of the population are descendants of the Jamaican workers brought to the banana plantation at the end of the 19th century. The only tourist attractions are the Museo Etnohistórico, recalling the landing in the bay of Columbus in 1502, and the Parque Vargas botanical garden.

The beaches of **Cahuita** are about 40 km (25 miles) south of Puerto Limón. A coral reef lies off Punta Cahuita. Access to the national park is from Puerto Vargas, a few kilometres to the south. Monkeys live in the humid forest. Further south again, swimmers will find fine beaches at **Puerto Viejo de Talamanca**.

The coast north of Puerto Limón is not served by roads. The only way to visit the villages is by boat on the coastal canal. Starting out from Moín or Hamburgo, this is the way to see **Tortuguero National Park**, 80 km (50 miles) to the north. This stretch of coast is an important nesting place for turtles to lay their eggs (late July to early October).

Dining Out

Costa Rica has an ample supply of fresh fruit and vegetables all year round. Beef is also of first-rate quality from the cattle farms of Guanacaste, as is the fish from coastal waters or from the mountain lakes.

Similar to Spanish tapas, small snacks called *bocas* or *boquitas* are served as an aperitif, often with a glass of good beer. They include *ceviche* (raw fish marinated in lime juice), chips, *frijoles* (black beans) or even turtle eggs, reputedly aphrodisiac.

Typical Costarican dishes are only lightly spiced and include rice, beans, sweetcorn, vegetables, meat, poultry or fish. There are also *tortillas*. The national dish of *gallo pinto* is mostly served at breakfast: rice, black beans and eggs, with a drop of sour cream and tortillas. For lunch, this speciality is cooked with the fried plantain bananas (*plátanos*), meat or fish and is then called *casado* (which means "married man").

On the Caribbean coast, local dishes are often prepared with coconut milk.

In the evening, soup is popular, whether it be an *ola de carne* cooked with beef, plantain bananas, corn and regional vegetables or a *sopa negra* with black beans and poached egg.

For dessert there is fresh fruit: such as mango, papaya, pineapple, banana and melon; or cooked desserts like caramel custard or coconut pudding.

Drinks

Try the delicious fruit juices, milk shakes (*batidos*) and of course the country's own excellent coffee. Wine is imported and expensive, but beer is locally brewed, as is rum (*ron*), gin (*ginebra*) as well as sugar-cane brandies (*cañas* and *guaro*).

Shopping

Costarican craftsmen produce beautiful leather goods. And don't feel you have to resist one of those typical colourful ox-carts from Sarchí. They are really well made, can be neatly dismantled for packing and are available in different sizes.

Also very attractive are the various carved wooden utensils and bowls, as well as hand-turned pottery.

Perhaps the most eye-catching and authentic craftwork of Costa Rica is to be found in the faithfully reproduced pre-Columbian jewellery fashioned from gold, jade or glazed obsidian.

And why not a packet of delicious Costarican coffee to bring back happy memories of a tropical breakfast?

PRACTICAL INFORMATION

Banks. They have different hours, depending on whether they are State banks (8.30 a.m.–3.30 p.m. on weekdays), or private (8 a.m.–6 p.m.)

Climate. The general climate of Costa Rica is tropical, but this changes according to altitude. In San José and over most of the Meseta Central, moderate temperatures prevail throughout the year; at higher altitudes, the temperature can drop below zero. The dry season *(verano)* lasts on the Atlantic coast from November to April, on the Pacific (Osa peninsula) two months less. During the rainy season *(invierno,* May to November) it will rain mostly in the afternoon and again at night, the mornings being quite sunny. This is also the hurricane season.

Credit cards. They are accepted almost everywhere in the country, even for small amounts. Visa and MasterCard are the most easily accepted, followed by American Express and Diner's Club. They can be used to withdraw cash from distributors.

Currency. The national unit of currency, the *colón* (plural *colones*) consists of 100 *centimos*. Coins: 5 to 500 *colones*. Notes: 1000 to 10,000 *colones*. US dollars and US-dollar cheques are widely accepted and can be easily exchanged for local currency.

Electricity. 110 volts AC, 60 Hz. Plugs have two flat prongs, like those of the United States.

Emergencies. Only one number for every emergency: 911.

Language. Spanish, partly English and Creole.

Safety. Costa Rica is probably the safest country in Central America. But it is not perfect — pickpockets practise their skills in crowded areas, and there is much petty thieving in the more tourist-ridden zones. San José's market district, the Caribbean coast and Puerto Limón in particular have a bad reputation. And don't go strolling there at night, especially not alone.

Time. GMT –6 hours.

Tipping. Apart from the big hotels and resort establishments used to dealing with North American clients, tipping is not very common in Costa Rica. In restaurants, the service charge (10 to 15%) is included in the bill.

El Salvador

EL SALVADOR

El Salvador is blessed with a verdant, mountainous landscape studded with majestic volcanoes and peaceful lakes. No fewer than 14 volcanic peaks form two ranks across the country. In the protective shade of leafy trees, coffee plantations cloak the fertile hillsides. Along the long Pacific coast, from Guatemala to Honduras, sandy beaches are the joy of sun-worshippers. Densely populated with 6.8 million people (90 per cent mestizo, 1 per cent full-blooded Indian stock), about a quarter is concentrated in greater San Salvador, the cosmopolitan capital.

San Salvador has few spots of interest, but it figures importantly, from the tourist's point of view, as a base from which to make forays into the beautiful countryside. At most, it's a few hours to anywhere in the country, aided by a good road network. Away from its bustle and chaos, smaller towns and villages seem a picture of the past, with cobbled streets, red-tile roofs and blazing-white colonial churches. The hardworking people have a creative bent, producing some original, attractive handicrafts.

The sun shines on this El Dorado landscape 360 days a year, with an average temperature of 27°C (80°F) in the capital. Perfect weather to enjoy water sports on the unspoiled coastline or mountain lakes, snake your way up a volcano or two, or visit some old colonial churches, Maya digs or colourful markets.

After years of bitter fighting, the Central American country of El Salvador has emerged from civil war and is mending its broken bones. A peace treaty was signed in 1992 under the auspices of the UN, and the subsequent election saw old foes take their seat next to each other in the legislative assemblies. Problems remain to be solved—there is still a vast gap between the many poor and the few extremely rich—but tourists sense the general will to surmount old difficulties and are quietly venturing back.

A BRIEF HISTORY

Pre-Columbian era
The Olmecs of eastern Mexico are known to have inhabited El Salvador as early as 2000–1500 BC, but most archaeological remains date from the Classic Maya Period (3rd to 9th centuries).

16th–18th centuries
In 1524 the Spaniard Pedro de Alvarado, fresh from his victory over Guatemala, begins a war of conquest against El Salvador, called at that time Cuzcatlán ("land of precious things"). In 1528, San Salvador is established at a site close to Suchitoto. In 1540 it is moved to its present site, receiving in 1546 the title of city from the Holy Roman Emperor.

19th century
The will to break free of Spain culminates on November 5, 1811, when Father José Matías Delgado rings the bells of San Salvador's La Merced church, calling for insurrection. After a long struggle, the Act of Independence of Central America is signed in Guatemala on September 15,1821. At first El Salvador joins with Honduras, Guatemala, Nicaragua and Costa Rica in the Provincias Unidas del Centro América, but the union is dissolved in 1839 and El Salvador becomes a sovereign independent nation.

In the second half of the century coffee replaces indigo as the chief export crop. Coffee cultivation leads to the peasants being pushed off their land to increase the size of the domains. The land falls into the hands of a mere 14 families.

20th century–present
In 1932, Agustín Farabundo Martí leads an uprising of destitute peasants and Indians; 30,000 are killed. In the 1970s civil unrest breaks out again, and the military usurp power. The murder of Archbishop Romero during mass in 1980 sees the outbreak of civil war. A stalemate is eventually reached between the rebels and the US-backed military, and the UN mediates a precarious ceasefire (1992).

Different guerilla factions form the Frente Farabundo Martí para la Liberación Nacional (FMLN) party to seek office through democratic elections. It has gradually gained representation, though the conservative Alianza Republicana Nacionalista (ARENA) party is the strongest political force.

Sightseeing

San Salvador

With more than 1.5 million inhabitants today, San Salvador was an obscure corner of the Spanish realm in colonial times and only in the 19th century did it rise to some importance. The city centre, damaged by earthquakes and polluted by vehicle exhaust, is a shadow of its former self. After the civil war, thousands migrated to the capital from the countryside and augmented the numbers of urban poor. The rich have abandoned the centre for the Escalón, San Benito and Santa Elena quarters to the west, where are found the upscale shopping centres and luxurious residences with high-tech security.

For a promenade in the city centre, let your landmark be the **Metropolitan Cathedral**, a huge, high-domed concrete church in Byzantine style, on the main square, Plaza Barrios. Its neighbour on the plaza is the imposing neoclassical **National Palace**, where the government had its seat until the 1986 earthquake damaged the building. It has been carefully restored and looks splendid. Behind the cathedral, to the east, is the **National Theatre**, which opened its doors in 1917, all opulently decorated with golden boxes, plush red velvet and grandiose ceiling frescos. It was damaged by civil

Dale Giesbrecht

Enlightened interior of El Rosario church in San Salvador.

war and earthquake but like the palace, has now been restored. Two blocks further east facing Parque Libertad is the modern **El Rosario church**, its soaring arched roof covering an interior adorned with figures made of scrap metal and a rainbow of stained-glass panels.

In the southwest part of town, the **Davíd J. Guzmán National Museum** displays some of the country's most important archaeological finds. Nearby is one of the city's loveliest churches, the **Basilica of La Ceiba de Guadalupe**.

More than 30 kinds of hummingbird have been spotted in El Salvador.

Claude Hervé-Bazin

The capital has some pleasant parks, including a botanical garden and a zoo, but the loveliest are outside the city limits. **Los Chorros Park**, 18 km (11 miles) northwest, features waterfalls and fern-covered volcanic cliffs, and **Balboa Park**, just 12 km (7.5 miles) to the south, has a network of trails meandering through forests and gardens, picnic areas and outdoor cafés. Just beyond Balboa is **La Puerta del Diabolo** (the Devil's Door), two monumental boulders on a summit, from where you have an excellent panorama over San Salvador, the surrounding volcanoes, and the town of **Panchimalco** below. Noted for its magnificent white colonial church, Panchimalco is the home of the Pancho Indians. A few still retain their old dress and traditions.

Around San Salvador

For boating, swimming or fishing, **La Libertad** is the closest beach, only 30 km (19 miles) from the capital, and appreciated by surfers for its high breakers. A little further to the east, however, are the best beaches in the country, a string of luxury resorts collectively known as the **Costa del Sol**. Another option for watersports is **Lake Ilopango**, in a giant crater resulting from a volcanic explosion in the 2nd century. It is just 15 km (9 miles) east of San Salvador.

East of Lake Ilopango is a trio of towns worth visiting. At **Cojutepeque**, walk up the hill to the large park containing a shrine to the Virgin of Fátima, who is said to have appeared in Portugal to three young children in 1917. Religious pilgrims come here from far and wide. The view from the top is superb. **Ilobasco** is renowned for its ceramics, and you can watch craftsmen at work at several places in town. **San Vicente**, in the midst of sugar cane country and at the foot of a volcano, has one of those blinding white colonial churches, its clock tower rising high above the town.

The West

Many cruise ships call in at **Acajutla**, home of a steelworks and a petrol refinery, both essential to the country's economy.

The largest city in the west of El Salvador is **Santa Ana**, a pleasantly provincial metropolis with an imposing neo-Gothic cathedral and a jewel of a theatre dating from the early 20th century. From here you can strike out to the south to some of the country's most noteworthy sights.

Beautiful, clean and crystalline-blue **Lake Coatepeque** occupies the crater of an extinct volcano. Steep wooded slopes rise all around, with the Cerro Verde, Santa Ana and Izalco volcanoes looming in the background. The

WORLD OF THE MAYAS

Along with Honduras, Belize, Guatemala and the Yucatán peninsula of Mexico, El Salvador forms part of the "Maya World", a touristic circuit linking the most important vestiges of meso-American history. The Maya peoples inhabited this region as early as 3,000 years ago under one common culture. El Salvador has several excavations in the circuit, impressive if not as spectacular as those in Honduras and Guatemala. Joya de Cerén was accidently discovered in 1976 by workers building a grain silo. In digging up the earth, they uncovered a Maya farmhouse community that had lain hermetically sealed under 5 m of volcanic ash since the year 600, when a volcano blew its stack. All sorts of everyday materials were found and are dis-played in a small museum: earthen-ware pots, knives and axes made of obsidian, grinding stones, pieces of jade, woven mats, and so on. Joya de Cerén is a UNESCO World Heritage site. The San Andrés ruins feature a step pyramid and various other structures, with more mounds to be excavated. Both Joya de Cerén and San Andrés are a half-hour's journey west of San Salvador.

Tazumal lies near Chalchuapa in the province of Santa Ana, 78 km (46 miles) from the capital. Its imposing pyramid rises to 23 m (75 ft). The Mayas practised a sort of ritual ball game here, as they did at Cihuatán, 40 minutes north of the capital.

locals adore their watersports here on the weekends and holidays, but quiet reigns weekdays. The popularity of the site has engendered a host of good restaurants and hotels.

High above the lake, at the summit of the old Cerro Verde volcano, **Cerro Verde National Reserve** has a front-row view of the Izalco volcano, which forms a black, bare cone of near mathematical perfection. It was active until 1957, when its fumaroles, which served as navigation guides for sailors, were suddenly extinguished (until then it was known as the "lighthouse of the Pacific"). Along the forested hiking trails, see how many of the 127 bird species you can spot—there are 17 kinds of hummingbird alone.

The East

Facing the Fonseca Gulf, the **El Jocotal** lagoon, festooned with water hyacinths, is colonized by thousands of ducks in winter.

In the northeast, **Perquín** was the headquarters of the FMLN rebels during the civil war. Their Museo de la Revolución Salvadoreña profiles the course of the conflict. On display are such horrors of war as homemade bombs and mines, biographies of those who died in action, photos of the grinding poverty that motivated the revolutionaries.

Dining Out

The capital has the most to offer, not only good, simply cooked steaks and seafood and indigenous dishes, but a choice of foreign cuisines and the inevitable fast-food spots.

For the simple food of the people, nothing is more beloved than *pupusa*, available from street stands or specialist *pupuserías*. The thick corn tortilla, filled with sausage, cheese or beans, is tasty, filling and inexpensive; a cabbage salad is the usual accompaniment. Another traditional dish is *sopa de patas* (beef feet and tripe soup), a spicy broth enhance by the addition of corn, potatoes, cabbage, yucca, tomatoes and plantain. Chicken appears in many guises, such as *pollo al achiote* (a tomato-based dish spiced with the powdered seeds of the achiote fruit), or *gallo en chicha*, stewed with tomatoes, carrots, plums, olives, potatoes, chickpeas, and pork sausages.

In the region of Coatepeque Lake, savour the crab soup and the freshly caught *mojarras* and *guapotes* fish. Most impressive of all in the seafood genre is a speciality of the eastern part of the country, the classical *mariscada*, a selection of lobster, crab, shrimp, oysters and fish simmered together in a delicious fish stock.

Claude Hervé-Bazin

The exotic fruit juices are luscious, but make sure they're not diluted with tap water; bottled fruit drinks or the local beer may be safer. Although coffee is grown everywhere, the brewed potion isn't very flavourful. Wine is available in luxury resorts, but is expensive.

Shopping

Salvadorans know how to turn the utilitarian and domestic into a decorative *tour de force*. The crafts of La Palma are famous throughout the country: woven textiles, toys and other objects carved out of wood, ceramics, leather articles, all charmingly painted in bright colours. Ilobasco pottery, especially the miniature dolls, is renowned.

Other appealing items are embroidered clothing and linens, gaily designed beach towels, a lifelike toucan or other exotic bird, hammocks or basketwares. For small souvenirs, the irresistible clay *sorpresas* (surprises) can't be trumped: open the walnut-sized shell, and inside is an elaborate arrangement of miniature figures—a nativity scene, for example.

San Salvador's markets, Mercado Nacional de Artesanías and Mercado Cuartel, showcase the wares of the whole country; haggling is expected.

PRACTICAL INFORMATION

Banks. In San Salvador banks open Monday to Friday 9 a.m.–1 p.m. and 1.45–4 p.m.; some also open Saturday 9 a.m–noon. Some banks have ATM machines.

Climate. Hot and subtropical climate, with relatively little seasonal variation. The coast is especially hot, approaching 35°C (95°F) maximum in March, but San Salvador, at 680 m (2,230 ft) above sea level, and higher mountainous regions, enjoy a more temperate climate. The rainy season is between May and October and the hurricane season from June to November.

Clothing. Lightweight cottons are recommended, and rainwear all year round. Modest clothing should be worn by women in this conservative Catholic country.

Currency. The national currency is the *colón* (colloquially called the *peso*), divided into 100 *centavos*. Coins from 1 centavo to S¢1, notes from 5 to 200 S¢. The US dollar can also been used, along with most of the major credit cards — check beforehand with your credit card company about availability of services. US dollars and travellers cheques may be exchanged at banks and bureaux de change *(casas de cambío)*.

Post Office. Monday to Friday 9 a.m.–4 p.m. ANTEL telecommunications offices keep the same hours.

Safety. Follow the example of Salvadorans and do not walk around after dark; take a taxi instead. Leave valuables in a hotel safe, or if you must carry them with you, they are safer in a wallet hidden underneath clothing than visible in a money belt.

Shops. Monday to Saturday 8 a.m.–noon and 2–6 p.m.

Photography. Do not attempt to photograph military areas.

Tipping. Restaurant bills do not include service charges, so 10 per cent should be given to the waiter, or even 15 per cent for a small bill. It is not customary to tip taxi drivers, unless they have provided a special service such as carrying your luggage.

Water. For drinking, stick to bottled mineral water.

Guatemala

GUATEMALA

As soon as you set foot on Guatemalan soil, you'll sense the weight of the country's history, forged by turmoil and strife. Against the forces of nature: many of the 33 volcanoes of the Sierra Madre are still active. And against the forces of mankind. The remnants of the mighty Maya civilization were far outmatched by the firearms, shields and horses of the Spanish conquistadors.

Stretching from the Pacific to the Caribbean, Guatemala is the most densely populated country of Central America, with over 13 million inhabitants. About 60 per cent of the population are *ladinos* (of mixed ancestry) or European, while 40 per cent are of Mayan origin *(indígenas)*. Devoutly religious, their Catholicism is but a thin veil cast over ancestral beliefs, profound mysticism and sacred rites. The brilliance of their costumes rivals the plumage of the quetzal, the sacred bird of the Mayas, whose name has been used for the national currency. Emerald green with a flash of white, the quetzal is said to have acquired his scarlet waistcoat when Tecún Umán, leader of the Quiché Indians, was killed in a duel by Alvarado. The bird lay on his breast and was forever stained with the blood of his wound.

If the Indians were no match for the conquistadors, the land itself rebelled with all its might. The Agua volcano made short work of the first colonial capital, engulfing it in a blanket of lava. The second, built a short distance away, was destroyed by earthquake and flooding. Another city (now called Antigua), set in the Panchoy Valley in 1543, survived more than two centuries. Razed by earthquake in 1773, it was left in ruins, its treasures salvaged and carried 45 km (28 miles) to the site of today's capital, Ciudad de Guatemala.

Strangely, the most seductive images of this country relate to its devastation: the ruins of Antigua; the lost cities of the Mayas; the smoking. mist-mantled volcanoes mirrored in Lake Atitlán; and the fierce pride of its resigned, resilient people.

A BRIEF HISTORY

Early times
The influence of the Olmec society, flourishing in the region of Veracruz (Mexico), spreads to Guatemala, El Salvador and Costa Rica. The Pre-classic then Protoclassic Maya periods end around AD 300.

4th–9th centuries
Classic Maya period. The civilization covers most of Central America. It reaches its zenith in the Petén region of Guatemala, especially Tikal. The Mayas study mathematics and astronomy, develop art and architecture, commerce and literature, using a complex written language.

10th–15th centuries
The great Maya cities are abandoned and the civilization declines.

16th century
In 1523, Pedro de Alvarado, under Hernán Cortés, invades Guatemala. He founds a capital, Santiago de Los Caballeros de Guatemala, in 1524 and moves it to the foot of Agua volcano in 1527. In 1541 Alvarado is killed in Mexico; his widow appoints herself governor but 3 days later the Agua volcano erupts, killing her and all but 75 of the inhabitants.

17th–18th centuries
The new capital in the Panchoy Valley (now Antigua) is the first planned city in the Americas. It suffers frequent earthquake damage and is finally reduced to rubble after a massive tremor on 29th July 1773. Another capital is built in the Ermita Valley, Ciudad de Guatemala.

19th century
Guatemala gains independence from Spain in 1821 together with the rest of Central America. In 1847 it is declared an independent nation. Coffee becomes the main export.

20th century–present
President Jacobo Arbenz Guzmán is overthrown in 1954 and for 30 years the army rules. Thousands of Indians are killed during the government's "anti-terrorist" campaign; 100,000 flee to Mexico. Scattered guerilla activity continues on a small scale to 1996. Antigua is declared a national monument in 1972. However, another earthquake strikes in 1976, killing more than 24,000 and leaving a million homeless. In the early 1990s La Ruta Maya (the Maya Route) is created, covering Yucatan, Belize and Guatemala, in an attempt to protect Maya interests.

Sightseeing

Guatemala City

Linked to North and South America by the Pan American Highway, the capital of the Republic of Guatemala was built only two centuries ago on a superb site, on the edge of a plateau. Because of earthquake damage, most of the buildings are recent, or have been heavily restored.

If you have a head for figures you'll soon get used to the street-numbering system, where *avenidas* run north to south and *calles* east to west. An address written 4a Av. 8-12 means 4th Avenida, between 8th and 9th *calles*, building number 12. Keeping the even numbers on your right-hand side, you'll be walking towards a higher-numbered *calle*. The city is also divided into zones; Zona 1 being the centre, where you'll find most of the sights. The museums are mostly in the southern districts (Zona Viva, 9, 10 and 13, near the airport).

Start your city tour at **Parque Central**, made up of Parque Centenario and Plaza de Armas, flanked by several imposing buildings. On the north side, the green granite **Palacio Nacional**, seat of the government, was built on the orders of General Jorge Ubico Castañeda, president from 1939 to 1943. On a guided tour you can admire the wood-beamed ceilings, sculpted columns, stained-glass windows and the numerous murals by Alfredo Gálvez Suárez, illustrating the history and culture of Guatemala.

On the east of Central Park, the huge **Catedral Metropolitana**, begun in 1782 and damaged by earthquake, may not look particularly inviting, and the interior is rather plain. However, many of the colonial and religious treasures salvaged from Antigua are housed here. The **Archbishop's Palace** to the left of the cathedral is one of the rare buildings to have been spared by tremors.

In the block behind the cathedral, **Mercado Central** is a new market built below street level since the devastating earthquake that occurred in the city's Jubilee Year, 1976. You'll find a good selection of Guatemalan handicrafts here, but not worth buying if you're heading for the village markets. (There's also an outdoor handicrafts market in the Parque Aurora.)

For a good view over the city, climb up to the **Ermita del Carmen**, northwest of Central Park. From this small 17th-century chapel, rebuilt since 1976, you can see two other churches, La Merced, crowned with a dome, and Santo Domingo.

You may find it hard to believe, but from one spot in Guatemala City you can look down over the whole country. In Parque Minerva, Zona 2 (north of the Palacio Nacional) a scale model, 36 m by 72 m, shows its topography in minute detail, with towns and villages marked by little flags. Francisco Vela, the engineer responsible for this **Mapa en Relieve**, travelled the land by donkey in 1904 to collect his data.

South of Parque Central, in Zona 4, the **Centro Civico** (1962–66) is claimed to be "the most advanced architecture in Latin America". Inguat, the tourist office, is here. Often inspired by Maya architecture, the modern buildings make use of the latest techniques in anti-earthquake technology. Several are decorated with frescoes, mosaics or other works of art.

Capilla de Yurrita, Ruta 6 8-52 in Zona 4, is one of the most amazing monuments in the city. Of pink-painted concrete, this chapel incorporates just about every style imaginable: Venetian balconies, Gothic porches and gargoyles, twisted pillars, the twelve Apostles peeping out of the windows. The chapel is privately owned, but you are allowed to enter: the interior is as opulent as the extraordinary façade.

In the southern part of town, in what is called the Zona Viva, you'll find the museums. **Museo Popol Vuh**, 6a Avenida, Calle Final, houses a private collection of Maya art, as well as colonial, religious and secular art and archaeological artefacts. The museum, on the campus of the Francisco Marroquín University, is named after the sacred painted book of the Quiché Maya. Only a copy can be seen here; the original is in Germany, and is known as the Dresden Codex.

The nearby **Museo Ixchel de Traje Indígena** illustrates traditional Guatemalan weaving as well as ceramics, jewellery and painting.

Just south of Parque Aurora, near the museum of modern art and the natural history museum, learn all about the ancient Maya in the fascinating **Museo Nacional de Arqueología y Etnología**. Apart from collections of stone carvings, ceramics and masks, there is a room displaying beautiful jade pieces, and a glass rotunda showcases the types of dwellings used by the Indians.

The nondescript ruins of **Kaminal Juyú**, Zona 7 in the suburbs, can be reached by bus. This Maya city dates from the preclassical period, before the rise of Tikal, and was discovered in the late 18th century.

When the citizens of Guatemala City want to relax, they head for the Pacific Coast, where, between the Chiquimulilla Canal and the ocean, a strip of black volcanic sand is brightened up by bars and swimming pools. One of the more pleasant ports is **Iztapa**, a few miles east of Puerto San José, like a desert island during the week but carnival-like at weekends. If you hate crowds, take a boat or walk to **Balneario Likín**, which has a quieter beach.

Antigua

Some 45 km (28 miles) southwest of Guatemala City, the former capital has remained more or less in the state the 1773 earthquake left it—rather less, as the earthquake of 1976 also took its toll. But few fail to recognize the crumbling city's undeniable charm. During Holy Week (the week preceding Easter) processions wind daily through the streets. Three volcanoes overlook the city, Agua, Fuego and Acatenango.

In the centre of town, arcaded **Parque Central**, the former Plaza de Armas, has seen corridas and tournaments; here too, people were flagellated or condemned to death. On the south side of the square, the **Palacio de Gobierno**, built in the 16th century, was damaged several times by earthquake. The façade survived, inscribed with the insignia of the Bourbons. The restored building now houses police and government offices, including the tourist office.

The **Metropolitan Cathedral** on the east side, was built in 1669 on the site of the city's first cathedral. Only two chapels are left, and behind them a jumble of broken arches and fallen columns. Bernal Díaz del Castillo, a 16th-century conquistador, is buried in the crypt.

The Universidad de San Carlos de Borromeo, built in the 1760s, has survived the tremors. It's a beautiful building, with a patio surrounded by an arched corridor and ornate plasterwork. It houses the **Museum of Colonial Art**, displaying collections of paintings, sculpture and ancient maps.

Of Antigua's many churches, the finest is **La Merced**, a few blocks north of Parque Central. Every inch of the façade, completed in 1767, is covered with stucco work, luxuriant flowers and vines, and lavish geometric patterns.

The **Convento de las Capuchinas** was built in 1737 for nuns invited here from Madrid, and is quite well preserved, with an arcaded courtyard. It is now used for temporary exhibitions of modern art.

The church of **San Francisco**, begun in 1544 by a Franciscan friar, expanded to cover four city blocks. Only one chapel survived; it was restored in the 1960s and, happily, resisted the 1976 earthquake. The remains of Hermano Pedro de Betancourt are buried in the crypt. This Franciscan monk, who established a

Traditional dress brightens up daily life in Santiago Atitlán.

hospital for the Indians in Antigua in 1650, was canonized in 2002; people still pray to him to heal their ills. Two streets to the north, **Casa Popenoe** has beautiful 18th-century interiors.

The **market**, on a site near the bus station, is an excellent place to buy textiles and embroidered blouses. North of here, the **Museo del Tejido** displays traditional costumes from the neighbouring villages.

Lake Atitlán

Smooth as a mirror in the morning, ruffled by the breeze in the afternoon, Lake Atitlán is Guatemala's most beautiful natural feature, 130 sq km (50 sq miles) in area. Along its southern edge, three volcanoes stand watch with their heads in the clouds: San Pedro, Tolimán and Atitlán, the highest at 3,535 m (11,598 ft).

The main base for hiking is **Panajachel** on the north side of the lake. With perfect weather year-round, a scenic location, and quiet beach, this makes an ideal base for boat trips to the picturesque villages on the shore and up on the hillsides.

Sololá is the provincial capital, founded in 1547 on the site of a Maya settlement. It's worth coming in on a Tuesday or a Friday for market day; otherwise there's nothing much of interest apart from the very ornate cathedral. But don't miss the annual festival, if you happen to be in the neighbourhood on August 15.

In **Santiago Atitlán**, on the southern shore, the women wear *huipile,* blouses embroidered with flocks of birds, and extraordinary headdresses, great lengths of woven cloth wound round and round their heads like top-heavy haloes. The corn god, Yum-Kax, is remembered in the church (1541); you'll note corn figures on the carved pulpit. Every year, the statues of the saints are cloaked in new shawls, embroidered by the village women.

Above Panajachel, **Iximche** was the capital city of the Cakchiquel Maya, founded around 1450. Perched on a promontory, surrounded on three sides by ravines, it escaped destruction after the Cakchiquel were defeated by the Spaniards. There's a small museum and several pyramids, on some of which you can still detect the original painted stucco.

A spectacular road leads to **Chichicastenango**, 40 km (25 miles) north of Panajachel. It's a quiet place of 10,000, except on Thursdays and Sundays when all the foreigners in Guatemala seem to home in on the famous market. This is where you find the best choice in local textiles, and glimpse the deep-founded pagan beliefs that still permeate the daily lives of the Quiché Maya. Near the flower-sellers on the steps of the church of Santo Tomas (1540), you'll see *chuchkajau*, witch-doctors, chanting and swinging primitive homemade censers over women kneeling in prayer, sending heady blue clouds of smoke above the heads of vendors and shoppers.

Near the church, the small Museo Regional houses numerous Maya artefacts, given in gratitude by the Indians to Father Rossbach, priest of Santo Tomas for almost 40 years in the first half of the 20th century.

You can walk up to the Shrine of Pascual Abaj on the outskirts of town, a carved stone head surrounded by altars. The idol is still worshipped with chants, prayers and incense.

At **Zunil**, up on the mountain slopes, the women swathe themselves in cloaks of all shades of pink and purple. In a house behind the church resides the strange god Maximón, a masked, fully dressed effigy sitting on a chair (he is probably the Maya god Mam). The Mayas firmly believe he can heal the sick, and ask for his favours by blowing cigar smoke into his face and pouring spirits into his mouth. **Fuentes Georginas**, just outside Zunil, is a hot spring sending up clouds of steam that waft through the fern fronds, making an exquisite picture.

Tikal

The extraordinary Maya site of Tikal, far in the north in the jungle-covered plain called El Petén, is best reached by plane from Guatemala City. The closest towns are Flores, on a small island in Lake Petén Itzá, and Santa Elena on the mainland, nearer to the airport, 64 km (40 miles) from Tikal.

The city lasted for one and a half millennia, until it was abandoned around the 9th century. Soon engulfed by the jungle, it lay forgotten by the outside world for centuries, though the old gods were still worshipped in secret. According to archaeologists, the

Maya Identity

Long before the conquistadors arrived, the Maya civilization had fizzled away, the splendid cities and temples obliterated by a thick carpet of jungle. Not so the Mayas themselves. Between 1524 and 1650, six out of seven of the Indian population were wiped out by fighting and disease. The survivors were reduced to slavery on lands conceded to the settlers. But the Indians maintained their own cultural identity. You'll recognize the same profiles in the cities and villages as on the ancient masks and carvings of Tikal and Quiriguá. The main food crop is still corn, the basis of Maya society and believed to be the origin of life.

site was occupied in the 7th or 6th centuries BC and reached its zenith around the year 800. But among the 3,000 buildings that have been mapped, the oldest date from the 2nd century BC.

Most of the structures are temples, palaces, shrines and ceremonial platforms; there are few domestic buildings, and it is not yet known whether this was only a ceremonial centre or an industrious, commercial city. A National Park since 1955, the site has two **museums**, one displaying the oldest stela discovered at Tikal, dating from AD 292, and the other a reconstruction of the tomb of the ruler Ah Cacao, who built many of the city's monuments around AD 700.

The heart of the city is the **Great Plaza**. Along the north side, a row of carved stelae relate the history of Tikal in hieroglyphs and illustrate the development of Maya art in their varying styles. The large complex behind them is known as the **North Acropolis**, where the remains of some of Tikal's ruling families were discovered. Sixteen temples are visible but many earlier buildings lie beneath. The **Central Acropolis**, on the south side of the square, is a labyrinth of residential and administrative structures along the palace reservoir.

The **Temple of the Great Jaguar** (or Temple I) closes the east side of the square. A jaguar is carved into one of the lintels. The nine-terraced structure, topped by a small temple, is one of the most impressive monuments of the site. The skeleton of Ah Cacao was found entombed in the vault, surrounded by ceramics and jade jewellery. Facing Temple I, the **Temple of the Masks** was also built by Ah Cacao and was named after the sculptures on its façade.

Of Tikal's seven great temples, the largest is Temple IV, of the **Two-headed Snake**, west of the Great Plaza at the end of the Tozzer Causeway, its peak high

The magnificent high temple overlooking the Great Plaza in Tikal.

above the tree tops. The tallest building of the Maya world, at 65 m (212 ft), it was built from limestone blocks, quarried from the rocks surrounding the temple and carved with obsidian blades. It's overgrown with vegetation, but by using roots to help you up, you can climb to the summit for a wonderful view of the city and jungle, home of howler monkeys and ocelots. Down below you see the Mundo Perdido, Temple III and partly excavated Temple V.

Eastern Guatemala

Puerto Barrios, the main port of the region, is the last town on the Atlantic Highway. From here you can take a boat to **Lívingston**, in its heyday the greatest port of Central America, but now a lazy place, a Black Carib (Garífuna) enclave almost entirely cut off from the rest of the country. Saturday night is reggae night in Lívingston, when the air throbs to the Carib beat. As the town—in fact it's more like a village, with painted wooden houses and coconut groves—has only two streets, you won't have to go far to find out where the action is.

The Maya ruins of **Quiriguá** lie 107 km (67 miles) west of Puerto Barrios, in the middle of a park surrounded by banana plantations. Unlike Tikal, Quiriguá is not noted for its temples but for the unusual carved stelae and

intriguing zoomorphs, huge rocks sculpted in the shape of toads, jaguars, snakes and mythological monsters. These original works were sculpted in the second half of the 8th century, after the emancipation of Quiriguá which was long subject to the city of Copán in Honduras, just over the border. The stelae, grouped on the central plaza beneath a roof of palm fronds, relate the history of the city and the genealogy of its rulers, of wars, politics, marriages and deaths. Stela E, fairly close to the entrance, is the tallest carved stone found in central America, 10.7 m (35 ft) high and estimated to weigh 65 tons. Both front and back are sculpted with the figure of a man holding in his right hand a sceptre depicting a long-nosed god.

At the mouth of Lake Izabal, the **Castillo de San Felipe** was built by the Spaniards in 1652 in a vain attempt to ward off pirates lured by the conquistadors' gold. It was restored in the 1950s and has become a popular weekend destination for hundreds of Guatemalans who enjoy its beautiful setting amid the palm trees. You can explore the maze of tunnels winding through the dank dungeons.

A 30-minute boat ride downriver takes you through walls of tropical forest to another lake, **El Golfete**. On its north shore, the

Biotopo Chocón Machacas is a nature reserve officially designed for the protection of the manatee. You may not spot one of these timid animals, who like to hide out submerged in the river, but there are plenty of butterflies, leaf-cutter ants, birds and interesting flora, and a museum.

Some 290 km (180 miles) from Puerto Barrios and 220 km (138 miles) from Guatemala City, **Esquipulas** at the Honduras border was an important trading and religious centre under the Maya civilization. Today it draws hundreds of thousands of pilgrims who come each year to venerate the Black Christ in the basilica. The statue, dating from 1594, is thought to have been sculpted in dark wood to resemble one of the Maya's own black gods, thus making the Christian symbol of the missionaries more acceptable to the Indians.

Dining Out

Guatemalan cuisine is similar to Mexican, basically black beans (*frijoles*), corn tortillas and rice. The national dish, *pepian*, is a thick stew of chicken, vegetables and roasted pumpkin seeds. Look for dishes with *chorizo* and *longaniza* sausages, *ceviche* (raw fish marinated in citrus juice until it is "cooked"), *pollo asado* (grilled chicken), pork in the guise of *lomo adobado*, beef grilled *churrasco*-style and *churchirto*, chopped meat in corn husks. Some of the vegetables readily available to accompany these dishes are *chirmol* (tomatoes), *plátanos fritos* (fried plantains) and *chojin* (radishes).

Lívingston is a gastronomic exception as you can expect to find Caribbean dishes. Favourites are *tapado* and coconut bread, accompanied by drinks known as *horchata* and *rosa de Jamaica* (and, of course, the local rum).

Shopping

Handicraft shops *(tiendas típicas)* in Guatemala City, Antigua and Panajachel offer wares from all over the country, but try to visit at least one village market. Best buys are the vibrant woven fabrics: each village has its own colours and patterns, geometric or covered with floral embroidery. Jade is sculpted into small objects and jewellery, mostly reproductions of ancient Maya and Olmec designs. They are not cheap, but the quality is high. (If you can scratch it, it isn't jade.) You'll find rustic clay pottery, leather goods and wood-carvings.

Antique shops in the cities sell colonial furniture, candelabra, carved chests and so on. Any pre-Columbian artefacts pushed for sale are probably fakes.

PRACTICAL INFORMATION

Banks. Open Monday to Friday 9 a.m.–3 p.m. (to 7 p.m. in Guatemala City), Saturday 9 a.m.–noon or 1 p.m. There are banks in all towns, but none at Tikal. Change foreign currency at a bank, preferably early in the day.

Climate. The coasts are hot and humid, El Petén hot and humid May to October, hot and dry the rest of the year. The highlands are generally pleasant and warm, but can be chilly during the rainy season, May to October. The hurricane season is from June to November.

Credit cards. The major international credit cards are widely accepted: MasterCard, VISA, Diners Club and American Express.

Currency. The Guatemalan currency is the *quetzal* (Q) divided into 100 *centavos*. Coins range from 1 centavo to 1 quetzal; banknotes from 1 to 100 quetzales. The US$ is also accepted and, in some cases, travellers cheques in US dollars. Re-change any local currency you haven't spent before leaving the country.

Electricity. The current is 110 volts AC, 60 cycles, as in the US.

Health. Insect repellent is a must on the coast and in the Petén. Be sure to remove the peel from fruit.

Language. The national language is Spanish; the Indians in the mountains speak various dialects derived from ancient Maya languages.

Post Office. The Central Post Office in Guatemala City opens weekdays 8.30 a.m.–5.30 p.m., Saturday 8.30 a.m.–3 p.m. Other post offices open weekdays 7.30 a.m.–12.30 p.m. and 1–2.30 p.m., Saturday 8–11 a.m.

Safety. There is some guerilla warfare in the highlands but you are not likely to notice it as it is well away from tourist areas. Beware of pickpockets. Keep your money and important papers in a pouch under your clothes.

Shopping hours. Shops are generally open Monday to Friday 9 a.m.–12.30 p.m. and from 3–7 p.m.; Saturday 9 a.m. to noon. Shops catering mainly to tourists keep longer hours. A long siesta is the custom.

Time. Guatemala follows GMT –6, the same as Central Standard Time.

Tipping. In restaurants, leave 10 to 15 per cent. It is not necessary to tip taxi drivers.

Water. Do not drink tap water. Bottled mineral water is readily available.

HONDURAS

Straddling the Central American isthmus, Honduras is roughly triangular, with its long side along the Caribbean coast and its southern point on the Pacific. Its name is ascribed to Columbus, who, when leaving the north coast, apparently said, "Gracias a Dios que hemos salido de esas honduras" (Thank God we have left those depths). Tegucigalpa, the capital, is set firmly inland at the heart of the Sierra Madre mountains, densely pine-forested and riddled with abandoned silver mines.

The nation's second city, San Pedro Sula, in the north, is the gateway to a region of palm trees and beaches steeped in a torrid atmosphere, the fiefdoms of banana companies. Just offshore, light years away from the rest of Honduras, the Bay Islands (Islas de la Bahia) stretch along the north coast. Far to the east, the jungles and mangroves of La Mosquitia are the last, almost uninhabited frontier.

A population of over 7.4 million is scattered across the country's 112,088 sq km (43,625 sq miles). The nation presents two very different facets: a Latino heartland and the Afro-Caribbean coast. If 90% of the population are of mixed origin, there are also 7% American Indians and 2% blacks, in addition to the white descendants of the few Hispanic colonists, together with Palestinian Arab Christians, well-established in the business community.

In the past, Honduras has suffered from a chronic lack of stability. From 1821 to 1981, the country underwent 159 changes of government, was involved in 24 wars with one or more of its neighbours, and saw 260 armed revolts. Today it is experiencing a rebirth, with a more democratic outlook, prospering and opening up to visitors.

At the southern frontiers of the Maya world, Honduras has some of its most impressive vestiges. The pyramids and palaces of Copán bear witness to the grandeur of this ancient civilization and the genius of its artists and sculptors.

A BRIEF HISTORY

1000 BC

The first settlement laying the foundations of Maya culture sees the light of day in the region of Copán.

3rd–9th centuries

The Classic Age heyday of Maya civilization. Copán reaches the height of its power between 600 and 800. At the beginning of the 9th century, Maya city-states collapse with the depletion of natural resources.

16th century

In 1502, on his final voyage, Columbus lands on Utila Island, then in Trujillo Bay. After the conquest of Mexico in 1521, Hernán Cortés leads an expedition to Central America, sending in his lieutenants, Cristóbal de Olid, then Pedro de Alvarado to colonize Honduras. The American Indian chef Lempira resists but is assassinated during a truce. In 1539, Honduras is incorporated into the Captaincy General of Guatemala.

18th century

Around 1750, the Bay Islands fall into British hands. In 1797, they deport there a community of Black Caribs, slaves of mixed African and Caribbean Indian origin who staged a revolt on St Vincent Island.

19th century

In 1821, Spain gives up its American colonies. The collapse of the Federation of United Provinces in 1839 makes Honduras an independent country. The Bay Islands are incorporated in 1859 after the departure of the British. Tegucigalpa becomes the national capital in 1880.

20th century–present

Wars and revolutions mark the turn of the 20th century. The American banana companies, which control 80% of the country's arable land, support the oligarchy in power. In 1969, a football match between Honduras and El Salvador erupts into open warfare, leaving 2,000 dead. In 1975, the government falls into the hands of the arm. The CIA makes Honduras its operations base in the fight against the Sandinista rulers of Nicaragua and the guerrilla warfarers of El Salvador. The country recovers a semblance of stability in the 1990s. Successive democratically elected governments launch programmes of social and economic reform. Elections are contested mainly by the pro-business Liberal and Nationalist Parties, with the Liberals' Manuel Zelaya winning the presidency in 2006.

Sightseeing

Tegucigalpa

More commonly known as Tegus to its residents, Tegucigalpa (Silver Hills) was in colonial times an important mining centre. The nation's capital (since 1880) is located at an altitude of 975 m (3,199 ft) in a basin surrounded by pine-forested mountains. Its construction development has been anarchic, first along the Río Choluteca, then climbing the hillsides. South of the river, Comayagüela, Tegus's popular alter ego and originally a separate town, has now merged with the capital—to bring the present population close to a million.

The historic heart of the city, bustling with street vendors, is the shady **Plaza Morazán** (or Parque Central) stretching out at the foot of the charming 18th-century **cathedral**. Inside, notice the Baroque altar held aloft by two angels at prayer. On the esplanade, contrary to mischievous legend, the monument dedicated to Francisco Morazán is indeed an equestrian statue of the Honduran national hero, president of Central America's Federation of United Provinces in 1830, and *not* Napoleon Bonaparte's Maréchal Ney. Writers Eduardo Galeano and Gabriel Garcia Marquez have confessed they had invented the story that the statue was bought in a Paris flea market when French Revolutionary monuments were going cheap.

The churches of **Los Dolores**, near a small market, and of **San Francisco**, the oldest in Tegucigalpa (1592) are both worth a visit. Among the attractions of the **Parque Concordia**, northwest of the city centre, are reproductions of ancient shrines and stelae from Copán. Nearby is the **Museo Nacional de Historia y Antropología** (National Anthropology and History Museum). Housed in the home of President Julio Lozano, it traces the nation's story from its pre-Columbian beginnings to the saga of the mines, railways and American banana companies.

Transformed from a 19th-century hospital on Avenida Miguel Paz Barahona, the town's newest museum, opened in 2005, the **Museo para la Identidad Nacional**, is a high-tech audio-visual dramatization of Honduras' tortuous history.

Overlooking the town, the United Nations Park up on **El Picacho** hill offers fine views over the whole central valley. Continuing along a track towards Rancho Quemado, you reach one of the two entrances to **La Tigra National Park** (the other entrance is at the abandoned mining town of El Rosario). Several trails lead through the reserve's vast expanses of pine forest.

Stela A in Copán depicts Waxaklajuun
Ub'aah K'awiil, otherwise known as
18 Rabbit, with a crown of woven matting.

Claude Hervé-Bazin

Central Honduras

Within a radius of 30 km (18 miles) around Tegucigalpa, the mining villages of **Santa Lucía, Valle de Ángeles** and **Ojojona** date back to the days when the Spaniards were working the silver mines. Restored to recapture something of their old appearance, they make a pleasant stroll around the stone-paved lanes lines with red-tile roofed houses.

Capital of Honduras from 1537 to 1880, the old colonial town of **Comayagua** has retained vestiges of its past. Its late 18th-century cathedral has a finely detailed white Baroque façade. The Casa Cural, seat of Central America's first university, founded in 1632, has been transformed into the Museo Colonial, displaying four centuries of religious art.

In a pretty setting of tall mountains and tropical vegetation, **Lake Yojoa**, the biggest in Honduras, is known for its perch fishing. Families come here at the weekend for fish dinners at one of the many open-air restaurants along the lakeshore. Dominated by the peak of Cerro Santa Barbara, 2,744 m (9,000 ft), the region is rich in pre-Columbian remains on the site of Los Naranjos, first inhabited 3,000 years ago. You will also see the beautiful Pulhapanzak waterfall cascading from a height of 90 m (295 ft) into a jungle-clad canyon.

Copán

Close to the Guatemala border, the charming little colonial town of **San José de Copán** (also known as Copán Ruinas) is the gateway to the finest Maya ruins in the country—perhaps in the whole of Central America. Before starting your visit of the archaeological site itself, be sure to visit the town's very instructive little Museo Regional de Arqueología Maya located on the main square.

The charm of Copán is irresistible. Often referred to as "Maya's Athens", the city-state, situated at the southernmost limit of Maya civilization, was one of the most advanced in the field of astronomy. At its height, it extended over 24 sq km (9 sq miles) and must have been home to 15,000 inhabitants. Here you will see no overpowering monuments, just open spaces revealing ruins of harmoniously proportioned pyramids and temples, splendidly restored.

Just off a path in the woods, the monumental **Plaza Mayor** displays some of the finest stone-carvings in Maya history, as if it were a sculpture garden. All around the esplanade, a collection of well-preserved stelae pays tribute to the kings of Copán. Some, such as Stela C, still bear traces of paint. Carved under the orders of 18 Rabbit, as the 13th sovereign is known, in a style characteristic of the region, these portraits with their profusion of symbols and mythic creatures are veritable history books. They have enabled archaeologists to reconstruct the genealogy of the rulers and the main events of the city.

East of this main square, the **Ball Game** (*juego de pelota*) constituted an important social event. Nobles and sovereigns came to attend the competitions, sometimes placing high-stakes bets on the results. The rings located at the side of the court, through which players had to throw the rubber ball, take the distinctive form of parrot heads.

The construction of the **Hieroglyphic Stairway** (*Escalera de los Jeroglifica*), built against a pyramid, was undertaken in the year 743 during the reign of Smoke Shell. The 63 steps are carved with some 2,500 figurative inscriptions, which archaeologists suppose are a form of family tree relating the exploits of all the monarchs of Copán.

From the **Acropolis**, the view over the Plaza Mayor and the Ball Game court is remarkable. The altar of Temple 16 is carved with the symbols of 16 members of the Copán dynasty. Yax Pac, the last of them, died in 820. In one corner, a splendid sculpture depicts the head of Pauahtun, an old man who held up the planet earth, in Maya mythology.

Near the information centre at the entrance to the site, the **Sculpture Museum** is one of the finest devoted to Maya culture. In addition to the many sculptures excavated on the site, the main attraction is a painstakingly reconstructed replica of the 6th-century terraced two-storey Rosa-lila (rose-lilac) temple. In order to preserve it, the original remains buried underground.

Other important stelae scattered through the valley can be visited on horseback. Near the town of La Entrada, between Copán Ruinas and San Pedro Sula, the Maya site of **El Puente**, beautifully located in a corn-growing valley, has several funerary temples and aristocratic houses served by the Maya's intricate drainage system.

The Southwest

Two hours' drive from Copán, **Santa Rosa** is an old colonial town with cobblestone streets. From here you can branch out into the region upon which the American Indians have left their mark.

The Lenca Indian village of **Belén Gualcho**, tucked away in the mountains, is reached by a road winding through the coffee plantations. It is the site of one of the country's most picturesque traditional Sunday markets.

At the end of a rough track about 45 km (28 miles) southeast of Santa Rosa, **Gracias** was briefly the capital of the *audiencia* (judicial district) for Central America from 1544 to 1549. The town has long since become a sleepy backwater, but its several colonial churches are worth a look. You may like to pay a visit to the hot springs 6 km (4 miles) to the south, or to **Celaque Park** with its humid mountain peaks covered in vegetation. The wildlife here includes jaguar, ocelot and the colourful crested quetzal bird in a tropical setting highlighted by a majestic waterfall.

North Coast

In 1870, American pioneer Minor C. Keith began building a railway line in Central America. To make the project profitable, bananas were planted along the fertile coastal plain of Honduras. The country soon embarked on exports to the United States. In 1911, Samuel Zemurray, a *gringo* planter, was the first to finance the overthrow of the regime by another, more favourable to the expansion of the plantations. His little operation enabled the banana companies to grab 4,000 sq km (more than 1500 sq miles) of land. Thus was born the world's first banana republic. Powerful states within the state, the companies ran everything, decided everything, and influenced the government whenever they deemed it necessary. To this day, the whole north coast is covered with hundreds of plantations. Private preserve of the American United Fruit and Standard companies, the region is the world's Chiquita banana capital, producing more than a million tons every year.

Situated close to the Caribbean, **San Pedro Sula**, with its 516,000 inhabitants, is the first city of Honduras in terms of commercial activity. Founded in 1536 by Pedro de Alvarado, it has kept few historic memories of its past. The main square, at the foot of the great cathedral built in 1950, is pleasant to walk around. You may like to visit the Mercado Guamilto, where the Asociación Nacional de Artesanos displays its wares next to the market's fruit and vegetable stalls. From San Pedro, you can explore the surrounding countryside with a rustic ride on the little banana-plantation train.

In **Puerto Cortés**, the country's largest port, the freighters are loading up non-stop with bananas and other tropical fruit bound for Miami, New Orleans or Europe. As you get further away from town, the Caribbean beaches grow ever prettier.

A half-hour drive to the west, **San Fernando de Omoa** is Central America's most imposing fortress. Built in 1777, it was supposed to safeguard the cargoes of silver extracted from the Tegucigalpa mines from the attacks of British pirates.

East of Puerto Cortés, **Tela**, the old company town of United Fruit, has become one of the country's main beach resorts. Overlooking a superb beach, the company headquarters and management villas have been transformed into a luxury hotel. The Caribbean coast is dotted with little villages of the Garífunas—descendants of American Indian and Afro-Caribbean stock. At the heart of the **Punta Sal National Park**, the hamlet of Miami, between Monkey Lagoon and Tela Bay, has best preserved the people's traditions. In a port accessible only by sea, the fishermen lead a peaceful life in palm-frond huts under the shade of the coconut trees. In season, the sea turtles come to lay their eggs in the warm sands. In summer (European wintertime), thousands of migratory birds make their nests on the lagoon. **Punta Izopo Park** east of the bay is home to parrots, toucans, monkeys and alligators.

A few kilometres from Tela, **Lancetilla**, the world's second-largest tropical botanical garden, was created by United Fruit in 1926 as a research centre. A pleasant trail criss-crosses the park in which more than 200 varieties of bird have been listed.

Surrounded mostly by pineapple plantations and renowned for its nightlife, **La Ceiba** provides the setting for a big carnival in the month of May. Some 25 km (15 miles) to the west, the **Cuero y Salado Wildlife Refuge**, at the mouth of two rivers, was set up for the protection of the siren-like manatees—but is also home to alligators and monkeys. Extending along the banks of the Río Cangrejal to the mountains, **Pico Bonito National Park** preserves a large expanse of altitude forest. You can spot tropical birds galore, armadillos and, with a bit of luck, jaguars lurking among the trees. Along the sea coast, the villages of Corozal and Sambo Creek are home to the Garífunas.

In 1502 Christopher Columbus landed in **Trujillo Bay**, one of the deepest in Central America. Despite the hardships of the humid climate and isolation, the Spanish hung on here under constant attack from British pirates. In the remains of the old redbrick fort of El Castillo, the rusty old canons still point out to sea. But Trujillo Bay's main attraction is the vast beaches of white sand spreading out beneath the coconut trees. To the east, **Guaymoreto**, a large lagoon linked to the bay, has abundant wildlife and exotic vegetation.

In **Capiro y Calenturo Park** up in the mountains behind Trujillo, you will get a chance to observe (or at least hear) macaws and howler monkeys.

La Mosquitia

The name (the Mosquito Coast known to Americans) seems intricately bound up both with the insect and the Miskito Indians who inhabit the region. There are in any case very few of them left—the people, not, alas, the insects— in this vast expanse of rainforest and mangrove, extending for the most part south into Nicaragua, home to alligators and

a prime destination for lovers of adventure. Accessible only by boat or small aircraft, the region includes the **Río Plátano Biosphere Reserve**, a UNESCO World Heritage Site since 1980 and for many visitors the finest nature reserve in Honduras, along with **Patuca National Park**.

Bay Islands

Off the Honduran coast, the Islas de la Bahía offer an otherworldly setting of golden sands, blue, blue skies and turquoise waters. Roatán, Utila and Guanaja are the three main islands, in addition to countless smaller isles. The population, largely descendants of African slaves who intermarried with Carib Indians, retain a memory of the old days when British pirates and Spanish Conquistadors fought for control of the high seas. In the reign of Queen Victoria, Britain extended its protectorate to the islands, neighbouring Belize and over to Mosquitia. Here, English is still spoken and a faint nostalgia remains for the days when this heavenly little corner of the world owed allegiance to Britain's Queen. Not that the islanders are utopians. They know full well the appeal of their beaches and ocean depths, among the most beautiful in the world. They are quite happy to exploit their home as a major tourist attraction.

William Walker

In Trujillo's cemetery, a tomb bears the simple inscription: *William Walker 1860*. A fearless and unscrupulous adventurer, Walker was a doctor and lawyer born in Tennessee in 1824, who managed to set himself up as the dictator of Nicaragua from 1855 to 1857. Aiming to seize the whole of Central America and running it with slaves, he tried to invade Costa Rica. Defeated, he wandered around Central America and was repeatedly deported. From the Bay Islands he launched a last abortive attack, on Trujillo, and was captured by a British warship. He was executed by a Honduran firing squad on September 12, 1860.

Some 60 km (40 miles) long and never more than 8 km (5 miles) wide, **Roatán** is the largest of the Bay Islands and also boasts the most modern facilities. A highway runs the length of the island through the woods of its hilly backbone. The diving fraternity heads for the numerous bathing complexes tucked away in quiet little bays. The coral belt surrounding the island is an extension of the Belize barrier reef—second in size only to Australia's Great Barrier Reef—and offers exceptional opportunities for diving.

Public transport makes forays around the island from Coxen Hole, its main town and centre for the banks and shops. At Sandy Bay on the north coast, take a look at the lush tropical vegetation in the Carambola Botanical Garden. Within the precincts of Anthony's Key Resort diving centre, Roatán Museum traces the island's turbulent history. But most visitors come to fulfil their dream of swimming with the dolphins. The research centre, built by the hotel owner in collaboration with the University of Mis-

Scarlet macaw, the national bird of Honduras: a rainbow flashing through the jungle. | Garífuna woman at home in a Mosquitia village. | A welcoming church built by a mission group.

sissippi, is a permanent home for several dolphins living in semi-liberty. They swim around spacious, closed-off lagoons, each 1.5 ha, with occasional "excursions" out to the high seas.

When you get to the end of the road at West End, stretching along a sandy cove surrounded by hotels and restaurants, you have to continue on foot or by boat to the splendid beach of West Bay, regarded as Roatán's most beautiful. Diving, sea-kayaks, chartering vessels for cruises or game fishing—almost all the major water sports are available here.

Leaving Coxen Hole for the east, the highway passes French Harbour, the island's main fishing port. Zigzagging between the hills, the road offers fine views of the north and south coasts. A track cutting across the island leads to Oak Ridge, a small Afro-Caribbean community with wooden houses perched on stilts. Black Caribs (Garífunas) deported by the British settled in Roatán's oldest village, Punta Gorda, founded in the 18th century. Their descendants still quietly cultivate their gardens. The tarmac surface ends here. Beyond it, Camp Bay, reached more easily by boat, stakes its claim, along with Paya Bay, as one of the island's finest beaches. Further east, Port Royal, an old pirates'

lair, stands at the entrance to a park of the same name, protecting a mangrove area.

When Columbus landed here in 1502, he named **Guanaja** "the Island of Pines". Entirely covered with mountains and forests and surrounded by mangrove, it is practically deserted. In pre-Columbian times, however, the island was bustling with life. Testimony of this has been the discovery of numerous remains on the slopes of Marble Hill. Today, the few inhabitants seeking shelter from the mosquitoes are nearly all living at Guanaja Town—Bonacca—on a little offshore isle. The wooden houses on stilts cling to a crazy maze of lanes among a labyrinth of canals and bridges. Recently, the main island has branched out into luxury tourism centred on deep-sea diving. If you make an excursion into the interior, your efforts will be rewarded by the sight of a beautiful waterfall.

West of Roatán, **Utila** is the least hilly and rugged and also the least developed of the three main Bay Islands. It has barely more than half a dozen cars. Nearly half its land area is covered by impenetrable mangrove. Many people come here for its very reasonably priced diving lessons. Legend has it that the infamous pirate Henry Morgan hid his booty somewhere on the island, which makes it a prime target for apprentice treasure-hunters. You may prefer scuba diving in the warm, translucent waters of the Jewel, Pigeon, Diamond or Water isles.

Off the beaten track of tourist haunts, **Cochino Grande** and **Cochino Pequeño** are the favoured isles of a dozen strung out along the coast of La Ceiba. Access is by boat only, for rent at the Plantation Beach Resort. Unspoiled coral reefs, rambles around the nature reserve and bird-watching are the main attractions.

Dining Out

The Caribbean's abundance guarantees huge portions of shellfish and freshly caught deep-sea fish. At lunchtime, restaurants usually propose a *plato del día* (dish of the day), always moderately priced. On the Bay Islands, you'll find rock lobster and shrimp on the menu. Whitefish or shellfish soups *(sopa de caracol)*, often accompanied by coconut bread, are typical dishes of Garífuna cuisine. *Tapado*, much appreciated on the Caribbean coast, is a fish or meat stew with plantain bananas, manioc and coconut milk. *Pinchos* are shrimp or chicken kebabs.

In common with the rest of Central America, the cornmeal *tortilla* forms the basis of all kinds of tasty snacks, with cheese and fried beans. Members of the same cornmeal pancake family are *tamales*, *enchiladas*, and so on). Street-corner snack-stands are plentiful—if you don't mind the hygiene risk. This is especially true for drinks. Stick to mineral water and bottled juices or sodas.

Shopping

Honduran craftsmen turn out a great range of quality products at very reasonable prices. You will see many stands along the highways, but in the major cities there are also craft markets selling wares from all over the country.

You will find leather goods (before you buy, make sure the leather has been tanned), musical instruments, embroidery, hammocks, silver jewellery and basketware. Ceramics, hand-made in the southwest of the country, are brightly coloured. Pots from Ojojona, a village high up in the mountains, are distinctively gourd-shaped and decorated with the head of a cockerel. You may also find copies of Maya statuettes.

On the Caribbean coast, the Garífunas use coconut and sea shells as a raw material for their ornaments. Honduras is also known for its cigars, rum (Flor de Caña) or fine coffee.

PRACTICAL INFORMATION

Banks. Open Monday to Friday 9 a.m.–3 p.m. American dollars and dollar travellers cheques are most easily changed. Euros and Canadian dollars are gaining acceptance in major cities.

Climate. Tropical. The rainy season starts in May and continues to October. It is cooler in Tegucigalpa. Hurricanes can hit the Caribbean coast between June and November.

Credit cards. Most hotels, restaurants and larger shops accept the major cards. Money can be withdrawn at banks with a Visa or MasterCard.

Currency. The local unit of currency is the *lempira* (L), named after a 16th-century American Indian hero, divided into 100 *centavos*. There are coins from 5 to 50 centavos and notes from 1 to 500 lempiras.

Electricity. Enquire at the hotel reception before plugging in an electric appliance, since Honduras uses both 110 and 220 volts AC, 60 cycles, the former being by far the most common.

Health. It is recommended to take anti-malaria medication. Be sure to pack an anti-mosquito product.

Language. Spanish is the official language of Honduras. Along the north coast and on the Bay Islands, English is spoken by most of the black population.

Opening hours. Shops normally open Monday to Saturday 8.30–11.30 a.m. and 1.30–5.30 p.m. The post office opens Monday to Saturday 8 a.m.–noon and 2–6 p.m.

Safety. Honduras is relatively safe, though it is advisable not to go out alone at night in the towns, especially in Tegucigalpa. Beware of pickpockets in crowded places and on the north coast beaches after nightfall.

Time. GMT–6, all year round. When it is noon in Honduras, it is 6 p.m. in London in winter and 7 p.m. in summer.

Tipping. Service is usually included in hotel and restaurant bills, otherwise it is usual to leave 10–15%. Porters and taxi drivers usually receive around 1 lempira.

Water. Tap water is generally not drinkable; beware of ice cubes.

NICARAGUA

Its strategic importance has often played tricks on Nicaragua. Variously the site for a canal projected to replace or parallel the Panama Canal, then a playground for great powers in their competition for regional influence, it was long regarded as little more than a banana republic, a useless pawn on the international chessboard. Repeatedly classified among the unstable countries, Nicaragua has now, like all its neighbours, regained a certain tranquillity.

With an area of 129,494 sq km, Nicaragua is at once the largest and least densely populated of the countries of Central America. Two-thirds of the 5.7 million inhabitants (of which 69% are *mestizos,* of mixed race) live in the towns built by the Conquistadores on the hot coastal plain bordering the Pacific. To the east stretches a line of volcanoes, several of which are still slumbering rather than extinct. Beyond them, the Sierra Madre rises to an altitude of over 2000 m. The rich volcanic soil, long abandoned as sterile, is once more producing coffee. The country's third geographical component in the interior, the Yapsi Tasba ancestral lands of the Miskito Indians, cover 40 per cent of the national territory, reaching all the way to the shores of the Caribbean. This is the region inhabited by the black and Indian minorities (9 and 5 per cent, respectively).

The land of Rubén Dario, one of Latin America's greatest poets, is slowly putting itself back together again. Injustices are still disturbing and poverty is rife, but unemployment has dropped from a high of 60 per cent in the 1990s to an official level of 3.8 per cent. Almost half the inhabitants are rated below the poverty level—though that, too, is a vast improvement on the 75 per cent figure of the 1990s.

Despite years of recurrent sadness and destitution, the people's good humour shines through. Nicaragua is a country of beautiful landscapes, impatient to find its place in the sun again.

A BRIEF HISTORY

10th century BC
A Nahuatl-speaking people of Mexican origin, the Nicarao, settle on the Pacific coast of what is now Nicaragua after the fall of Teotihuacán.

16th century
In 1522, an expedition from Panama, led by Gil González de Avila, reaches the southern shore of Lake Nicaragua. Two years later, the territory is occupied with minimum force by Hernández de Córdoba. The towns of Granada and León are founded that same year.

17th–18th centuries
The Caribbean coast becomes a prime target for English and French pirates. Granada is repeatedly plundered.

19th century
Spain grants independence to its colonies in Central America in 1821. After the failure of the Federation of United Provinces, Nicaragua becomes a nation in its own right in 1838. Britain and the United States show a growing interest in this little country as the possible site for a canal linking the Atlantic to the Pacific. From 1848 to 1860, La Mosquitia becomes an autonomous kingdom under British protectorate. In 1855, an American adventurer by the name of William Walker seizes power with the aid of the liberals of León. Aiming to take control of all the Central American countries, he runs into the resistance of Costa Rica and is finally driven out. At the end of the century, with the blessing of the local great families. American and British mining and agricultural companies increasingly become states within the state.

20th century–present
The United States intervene militarily in 1912, on the pretext of securing the strategic zone of a canal that will never see the light of day. It is also a matter of defending the interests of the United Fruit Company. The occupation lasts by and large till 1933. Troops led by revolutionary general Augusto César Sandino (a name later invoked by the Sandinista forces) try to drive the invaders out of the country. But Sandino is assassinated in 1934. Two years later, aided by the Americans, the Somoza clan seizes power. It holds on to it for the next 43 years, amassing a fortune at the expense of the people. The 1972 earthquake leaves 10,000 dead, and a large part of the international aid is embezzled by the Somozas. Founded in the 1960s, the leftist Sandinista National Libera-

tion Front (FSLN) organizes strikes and demonstrations supported by parts of the Roman Catholic clergy. In 1979, following assassinations and the bloody crushing of a popular insurrection, the regime of Anastasio Somoza is finally forced out. Sandinista leader Daniel Ortega takes power and institutes social, political, and economic changes, notably land redistribution, education and health care. But alliances with Cuba and the Soviet Union prompt the USA to arm counterrevolutionary contras. Their guerrilla warfare in the 1980s ends in stalemate. The Esquipulas peace agreements of 1987 lead three years later to moderate Violeta Chamorro becoming Latin America's first freely elected woman president. Liberal and often corrupt conservative leaders govern Nicaragua throughout the 1990s. In 1998, Hurricane Mitch devastates the country's agriculture, leaving 4000 dead. Daniel Ortega, defeated for the presidency in 2001, returns to power in November 2006 on a more moderate platform. With the support of the Roman Catholic Church, he pursues policies of what Latin America calls the soft "vegetarian left" rather than the hard "carnivorous left" of Venezuela's Hugo Chavez.

Sandino crushes Uncle Sam: mural paintings in León have been carefully preserved.

Claude Hervé-Bazin

A play of light and shadow in a street of Granada, whose buildings retain memories of the colonial past.

Claude Hervé-Bazin

Sightseeing

Managua

More than 1 million people, a quarter of the country's total population, live in the capital, which stretches along the southern shore of Lake Managua. It became the seat of government in 1857; located halfway between liberal León and conservative Granada, it represented an ideal compromise. The city was destroyed by a major earthquake in 1931, then rebuilt, only to be devastated again by the earthquake of 1972.

Its wide airy avenues and monuments to the glory of revolutionary heroes recall its involvement with the republics of the former Soviet Union, but new shopping districts have developed around the Nuevo Centro. From its colonial past, the town has retained the decaying yet splendid remains of its now roofless **Cathedral**, while the neighbouring **Palacio Nacional** has been nicely restored to house the National Museum. Together with the **Centro Cultural** built on the ruins of the old Gran Hotel, these are the only traces of the old historic centre. Nearby, you will see the modern buildings of the **Teatro Rubén Dario** on the way to the lake and the **Malecón** promenade, particularly lively at the weekend.

Further to the south, the **Loma de Tiscope** hill, guarded by a huge statue of Augusto César Sandino, overlooks the little crater lake and offers a panoramic view of the capital. Beyond it is the new and eye-catching multiple-domed **Metropolitan Cathedral** designed by Mexico-based Italian architect Riccardo Legorreta. It was built in only 16 months and completed in 1993.

To the southeast, the huge and friendly **Mercato Roberto Huembes** sells not only fruit and vegetables, clothes, hammocks and pirated CDs, but also includes a big section devoted to craftwork: paintings, jewellery, ceramics, and so on.

As for the rest, the town divides into popular neighbourhoods and prosperous suburbs—along Carretera Sur in particular. Since road names are not used very much, be sure to have a good town map with you to avoid having to ask your way too often. Otherwise, it's worth knowing that people will often direct you using as landmarks major buildings that were destroyed in 1972 but still loom large in their memories.

The region around Managua is dotted with crater lakes. Some 20 km (12 miles) to the northwest by the old León road, **Xiloá Lagoon** is one of the prettiest. It has been well developed as a much appreciated recreational area for families flocking here at the weekend.

León

Fierce competition has always been waged between León the Liberal and Granada the Conservative. Capital of the Spanish colony for more than three centuries and originally known by the grand name of *Santiago de los Caballeros de León* ("St James of the Knights of León"), this is the home town of Rubén Darío (1867–1916), the national poet. Its university, founded in 1804, and its religious schools have placed this city of 148,000 inhabitants at the centre of the country's intellectual activity. Nowhere more than here was the revolution of 1978 followed with so much fervour. On the walls of the houses you can still see several frescoes urging the people to fight.

Built in the Parque Central, the Baroque **Cathedral**, largest in Central America, was built here, in all its splendour, by mistake: it is said that its architectural plans were originally supposed to go to the construction of the cathedral in Lima, Peru. The foundation stone was laid in 1746, but the building was not completed till the 19th century. Notice high on the façade four (very slim) atlantes propping up the bell-niches. The interior's treasures of religious art recall the wealth of the Spanish colonial Church. Near the altar, a melancholy lion looks upon the tomb of poet Rubén Darío. A rooftop tour offers a splendid view over the city centre and the surrounding volcanic peaks.

Each quarter has its own church. Among the most interesting are **La Merced** with its great Baroque high altar, **El Calvario** east of the main city square, and **Subtiava** in the west part of town. Subtiava was erected in 1530, long before the town of León was built on its present site. Bartolomé de las Casas, who proselytized among the American Indians, preached there on many occasions. The colonial-era altar is regarded as the most beautiful in the country. However, none of these churches can equal the beauty of **La Recolección**, built in the late 18th century, on Calle de los Bancos. Its dark saffron yellow Baroque façade is decorated with a profusion of spiralling columns and a dozen primitivist bas-reliefs depicting scenes from the Bible.

On Calle Rubén Darío, the house where the great poet lived has been converted into a **museum** (closed Monday). It owns a large collection of his manuscripts, as well as many personal memorabilia. Closer to the Parque Central, the **Museo de Arte Fundación Ortiz-Gurdián** exhibits modern works by Nicaraguan and other Latin American artists.

Throughout the town, many sites commemorate battles of the 1979 revolution, such as **El Veinte Uno,** the notorious XXI prison of the pro-Somoza National Guard. It now houses the **Museo de Tradiciones y Leyendas** in which the cells exhibit various aspects of Nicaraguan folklore, along with paintings on the walls depicting the torture meted out to prisoners from 1921 to 1979. Rather less depressing, just north of the cathedral, are the remarkable **mural paintings** by Sandinistas illustrating the theme of national liberation—you may recognize Uncle Sam being crushed underfoot by Augusto Cesar Sandino.

León Viejo

Founded in 1524 some 30 km (18 miles) from the present-day site of modern León near Lake Managua, the country's first capital nestles at the foot of the Momotombo volcano. It was almost entirely levelled to the ground by the earthquake of December 31, 1609. Cleared of their coating of volcanic ash, the remains of the cathedral and a few other buildings are once again visible. The **Momotombo** reflecting its superb cone in the lake can be climbed with the help of a guide. The same is true of the **Cerro Negro**, the most recent basalt cone to form in the western hemisphere, which came into being in 1850.

Pacific Beaches

From León a road leads about 30 km (18 miles) to the long grey-sand beach of **Poneloya**. Deserted on weekdays, it's a great place to sunbathe in peace and quiet, but not good for swimming because the strong currents can be quite dangerous. Nearby, **Isla Juan Venado** is a nature reserve ideally explored in a sea kayak. Closer to Managua, the **Pochomil** and **Montelimar** *playas* also enjoy an excellent reputation.

Indeed, the whole Pacific coast offers a long string of good beaches. Not far from the border with Costa Rica, the fishing village of **San Juan del Sur**, at the edge of a pretty bay, is fast becoming Nicaragua's main beach resort, with facilities for game fishing. It was from here, in the 19th century, that gold-diggers bound for California got back on the boat after travelling by coach across the strip of land separating them from Lake Nicaragua. Several other beautiful beaches can be found along the coast. Among the finest are Marsella and Majagual, much appreciated by surfers, as well as Coco.

In the same area, the **Punta La Flor Reserve** is the most accessible of spots where sea turtles lay their eggs. From July to January, on moonless nights, they come in their thousands to lay their eggs in the lukewarm sands.

The Burning Mountain, Masaya Volcano, smoking in the distance beyond the calm waters of the lagoon.

Claude Hervé-Bazin

Matagalpa

The coffee plantation capital, due north from Managua, suffered considerably from the fighting during the revolution. Apart from a small museum dedicated to Carlos Fonseca, one of the fathers of the uprising, and another even smaller one devoted to the coffee industry, the town serves principally as a base for exploring the region.

Some 15 km (9 miles) to the north, the **Selva Negra** hotel organizes guided jungle tours to see the monkeys and ocelots. Similar facilities are available at **Finca Esperanza Verde**, a remote spot in the mountains 25 km (15 miles) to the east. A rough track leads through beautiful countryside to **Jinotega**, 34 km (21 miles) away. Its huge San Juan cathedral (1805), frequently rebuilt, has a profusion of religious treasures.

Masaya and the Pueblos Blancos

Located only 26 km (16 miles) east of Managua, just after the entrance to the Masaya Volcano Park, the town is known for its bustling, colourful **Mercado de Artesanías**. The market sells crafts from all over the country, as well as the nearby American Indian village of Monimbó. Closer to the middle of Masaya, the **Centro Cultural Antiguo Mercado** occupies a pretty market hall built at the end of the 19th century. But one of the best features of Masaya is the superb view over the Masaya lagoon and Santiago volcano. On September 30, spectacular dances in full Indian costume are staged around the Church of San Jerónimo to celebrate the feast day of the town's patron saint—a must for anyone in the region at this time.

A few kilometres from Masaya, the village of **Nindirí** has preserved the fine late-18th-century Church of Santa Ana, along with the interesting little Museo Tenderi, displaying pre-Columbian art. Beyond, several Pueblos Blancos (white villages) are worth a visit, among them **Catarina**, with its magnificent panoramic view of the **Laguna de Apoyo** crater lake, **Niquinohomo**, where the birthplace of Sandino has been converted into a library, and **San Juan de Oriente**, reputed for its pottery workshops.

Masaya Volcano

Created in 1979, the Masaya Volcano National Park, Nicaragua's first, covers 53 sq km (20 sq miles) of land dramatically scarred by lava flows and pierced by five craters. There are in fact two volcanoes in the park: the Nindirí and the Masaya—or Popogatepe ("Burning Mountain"). In pre-Columbian times, the Masaya was revered by

American Indians, and it's believed they sought to appease it by sacrificing children and young girls. Later, at the time of the Conquista, the Spanish climbed the volcano hoping to discover in it a vast cauldron of gold. Disappointed, they planted a cross on the rim of the crater as an attempt to exorcise this "Mouth of Hell". The most recent eruption of Nindirí dates back to 1670, and that of Masaya to 1852. On this occasion the new Santiago crater was formed between the two volcanoes. This has since repeatedly manifested itself, settling down finally in 1985 but still steaming.

Just beyond the park entrance, an information centre houses exhibitions devoted to the park's geology, flora and fauna. You will learn that the eruptions are of the "Hawaiian" type, that is to say, spewing out vast amounts of lava but not very dangerous. Although most of the animals roaming the park are nocturnal creatures (coyotes, raccoons, opossums, etc.), you may spot iguanas or monkeys. In late afternoon, the green parrots return to their nests located inside the crater, apparently unperturbed by the clouds of toxic fumaroles spouting out of it. During the dry season, the lava flows overgrown with vegetation are covered with flowers. The main road leads to the area of the Nindirí volcano at the foot of the Bobadilla Cross, from which the view extends over the whole region. There are also several hiking trails crisscrossing the park, and you can visit lava caves with a guide, a stunning experience.

Granada

Located at the far north end of Lake Nicaragua, at the foot of the Mombacho volcano, the country's historic conservative stronghold (population 92,000) was established in 1524 by the conquistador Francisco Hernández de Córdoba, and can claim to be the oldest city founded by Europeans in Central America. Thanks to its major port, reached from the West Indies and from Europe by the River San Juan, Granada became one of the richest cities in Latin America. In the 17th century it was subjected to repeated raids by English and French pirates and plundered for the last time in 1857 by the American adventurer William Walker. It nonetheless preserves magnificent traces from its opulent past.

Some distance from the lake, the majestic and spacious **Parque Central** is for many visitors the most beautiful main square in all Central America. Lovingly maintained, the buildings have a resolutely Castilian air about them. On the east side of the square, the **Cathedral**, first built in 1583, was destroyed by Walker and rebuilt in neoclassical style in 1915. To the north, the **Casa de los Tres Mundos** (House of the Three Worlds), a colonial mansion with a doorway guarded by two chained stone lions, is now a cultural centre. On the other side of the square behind the bandstand is the Hotel Alhambra, Granada's oldest. As a backdrop to the south, the cone of the Mombacho volcano looks down on the arcades of the attractive **Palacio Municipal**. Horse-drawn carriages wait in the shade of the trees to take visitors on a tour.

Take Calle Xalteva to the west to reach the Church of **La Merced**, inaugurated in 1783 and restored in the following century. Further along, you will find the churches of **Xalteva** and **La Pólvora**. Northeast of the Parque Central, the **Antiguo Convento de San Francisco**, built in 1524 when the city was founded, served as a garrison and university before being transformed into a museum. It exhibits 28 pre-Columbian sculptures found on Zapatera Island. Next door is the splendid San Francisco church.

Calle La Calzada passes the church of **Guadalupe** to reach Lake Nicaragua at Plaza de España.

Colourful facelift for a restaurant in Jinotega | Catch the ferry boat to Ometepe Island, formed by the merging of two volcanoes.

Claude Hervé-Bazin

Claude Hervé-Bazin

Claude Hervé-Bazin

Follow the waterfront promenade to the **Centro Turístico**. From here you can take boat cruises out to the 380 islets and miniature volcanoes scattered across the lake. One of them, **San Pablo Island**, is the site of a Spanish fortress built in the 18th century as an effort to protect Granada from the pirate attacks. Other excursions lead to the park of **Mombacho Volcano** where well-organized trails to the summit enable you to explore its high-altitude forest.

Lake Nicaragua

Largest of Central America's lakes with an area of 8,262 sq km (3,190 sq miles), Lake Nicaragua has the signal status of being the only known lake in the world to provide a home for freshwater sharks—a very rare species since Anastasio Somoza decided to exterminate them. The lake's strange aquatic universe is a legacy of the geological troubles that have marked the region. Originally a bay on the Pacific, the stretch of water was cut off from the ocean by the build-up of successive deposits of volcanic lava floes forming its western shore. Fed by over 40 streams and rivers, it gradually lost its salinity and its fish had to adapt to this new freshwater environment.

In the 1850s, this veritable interior sea formed a vital link between the Caribbean Sea and the Pacific Ocean. Steamboats going up the Río San Juan transported consumer goods to Granada and passengers heading for California—or on the return trip the bounty from the gold mines. From there, people and material continued by road across the narrow strip of land separating the lake from the nearby Pacific. For a long time, the route was a competitive alternative to the Panama isthmus for the construction of a trans-oceanic canal.

An hour's boat ride from Granada (rentals at the Centro Turístico), **Zapatera Island** in Lake Nicaragua is one of the country's principal archaeological sites. Impressive statues of animal figures have been found there dating between 600 and 1200. They have been transferred to the country's museums, but you can see the pre-Columbian tombs and rock drawings of the neighbouring **Isla del Muerto**.

A trip to **Ometepe Island**, the largest in Lake Nicaragua, takes an hour from San Jorge on the south shore, or 4 to 4.5 hours from Granada. Ometepe's landmark twin hills make it visible from afar. It was formed by the merging of two volcanoes, Maderas, 1,394 m (4,573 ft) and Concepción, 1,610 m (5,282 ft), which is still active today. Along its shores, several villages live from fishing and farming. The rich volcanic soil provides abundant crops of bananas, citrus fruits, coffee and cocoa.

A few buses ply between the villages, and you should always be able to find a taxi if you want to explore the island. Otherwise, rent a boat. You can hike to the forested upper slopes of the Maderas volcano, haunt of parrots and howler monkeys, to discover its crater lake. Climb the slopes of Concepción volcano with a guide, or relax on the grey sand beaches of Santo Domingo. You might also like to see out the ancient petroglyphs: many traces of the pre-Columbian era have been excavated in the countryside. Most of the sculptures, similar to those from Zapatera Island, represent humans, animals or geometric motifs, in particular spirals. Some are displayed in the Museum of Altagracia.

On the south side of the lake, the **Solentiname Islands** enjoy a matchless serenity that makes the archipelago a refuge much appreciated among Nicaraguan artists. A school of primitivist painting was founded here in the 1970s by Father Ernesto Cardenal, a progressive priest who participated in the Sandinista government. The island's other residents are fishermen. Pre-Columbian inhabitants have left their traces on these islands, with finds now exhibited in a small museum.

Río San Juan

An outlet for Lake Nicaragua, the river has long served as a transport route between the Caribbean and the Pacific. From the town of **San Carlos** at the entrance to the lake, boats journey down to the river's estuary at **San Juan del Norte**. The trip takes you at a leisurely speed through tropical forest—10 to 12 hours downstream, longer upstream. Many stretches of the river are protected areas, beginning with the huge **Indio-Maíz Biological Reserve**. On the way, you will see the imposing fortress of El Castillo, built by the Spanish in 1666 in an attempt to block attacks by the pirates.

From San Carlos, excursions are available to another major nature reserve, the **Parque Los Guatusos**, inhabited by monkeys, crocodiles, caymans, exotic birds and even a few jaguars.

Caribbean Coast

In the 18th century, the coast was the preserve of English or French pirates seeking a haven there. Never colonized by Spain, the territory, today an autonomous area, has remained mainly English-speaking. A region of tropical rain forest, Nicaragua's Atlantic coast is home to 100,000 American Indian Miskitos, Sumos and Ramas. Under the Sandinistas, some of them were forcibly displaced to the interior to prevent them allying with the *Contras,* and they took up arms against the government. In the coastal ports, other inhabitants are *mestizos* (mixed blood) settled here from the west or black descendants of slaves both from here or brought in from Jamaica. This remote region is accessible mainly by air or by boat coming down the Río Escondido from Rama to **Bluefields**. In the more swampy north, Río Coco, separating Nicaragua from Honduras, remains one of the only transportation routes.

A 75-minute flight from Managua takes you to Bluefields' two offshore Corn Islands, **Islas del Maíz**. With their translucent waters, coral reefs, coconut groves, game-fishing, diving and rock lobster, these islands present the Caribbean face of Nicaragua. The inhabitants have been here since the era of British colonization.

Dining Out

Nicaragua is a country of modest resources and humble fare. The staple dish is usually red beans and rice *(gallo pinto)*, accompanied by tortillas, cabbage salad and, for the better-off, chicken, pork, beef or fish. For a change of pace, you can always seek out the Chinese restaurants and others, more cosmopolitan, in Managua.

Among the local specialities, it is worth sampling *nacatamales*, balls of maize stuffed with chopped meat or vegetables and cooked in a banana leaf; *chicharrones*, fried pork rind; or *tajadas*, plantain banana chips. The latter are served lightly cooked *(maduros)* or fried with cheese *(tostones)*. On the Caribbean coast, particularly on the Corn Islands, be sure to try a rock lobster or the excellent *rundown*, a stew in coconut milk.

Shopping

One of the best places to do your shopping is the Roberto Huembes market in Managua, though some claim that Masaya is even better; there you will find all kinds of crafts made from cloth, hemp, leather and wood, together with attractive ceramics copying the pre-Columbian style made in nearby San Juan de Oriente. Make sure they are carefully wrapped. Bargaining for a good price is usually considered acceptable.

Nicaraguan craftsmen produce a wide range of household wares or ornaments. White cotton hammocks roll up to fit neatly into your bags. In addition, you will find attractive jewellery, basketware, wood carvings and leather bags, belts and shoes. Painters in the Solentiname Islands produce much appreciated primitivist canvases.

PRACTICAL INFORMATION

Banks. They are open Monday to Friday 8 a.m.–noon or 12.30 and 1 or 1.30 p.m.–4.30 p.m. (Saturday usually 8.30 a.m.–noon). Cash distributors (ATMs) are available, principally in Managua, León and Granada. Travellers cheques are rarely accepted outside the capital, but US dollars and increasingly Euros can quite easily be changed at currency exchanges and hotels in the major cities. Major credit cards are accepted in the big hotels.

Climate. The rainy season *(invierno)* lasts from May to October in the west and until January on the Caribbean coast (September and October risk of hurricanes). Temperatures vary with altitude. It's hot in Managua and on the Pacific coast (up to 40°C in March and April), cooler around Matagalpa. The hurricane season is from June to November.

Conservation. To protect an endangered species, you should not buy tortoiseshell goods, which are in any case banned from import in Europe and North America.

Driving. The main roads are often pockmarked with potholes. The smaller roads are sometimes very rough going in the rainy season.

Health. Take up-to-date anti-malaria medication, particularly if you are going to the Caribbean coast. And don't forget anti-mosquito products.

Money. The Nicaraguan unit of currency is the *córdoba* (C$), also often known as a *peso*, divided into 100 *centavos*. There are banknotes from C$10 to C$500 and coins from 5 centavos to C$5.

Opening Hours. Office hours are Monday to Friday 8 a.m.–noon and 2–4 or 5 p.m. Small supermarkets and shops often stay open to 8 p.m. Managua Post Office is open Monday to Friday 8 a.m.–5 p.m. and Saturday 8 a.m.–noon.

Security. It's a good idea not to go around alone in the Caribbean region (other than the Corn Islands). Otherwise, beware of pickpockets in the larger towns, especially in the busy markets.

Time. GMT –6. When it is noon in Managua, it is 7 p.m. summertime in London and 6 p.m. in winter.

Water. Stick to bottled mineral water.

Panamá

PANAMA

The name (more correctly Panamá) may sound Hispanic, but it is in fact an Indian word thought to mean "land of many fish", used by its indigenous people to describe their homeland long before the arrival of the conquistadors. Discovered by Spanish explorers in 1501, the isthmus acquired major strategic significance after the conquest of Peru. Vast quantities of Inca gold, and later silver from the mines of Bolivia, were transported by mule train from the Pacific to the Atlantic coast for shipment to Spain.

Forming the easternmost part of Central America, Panama occupies the narrow neck of land that stretches for 640 km (400 miles) between Costa Rica in the west and Colombia in the east. Its average width is 120 km (75 miles), and at the narrowest point it's a mere 50 km (31 miles) wide between the Atlantic and the Pacific. The country has flourished thanks to its strategic location at the meeting of all the great trade routes. Apart from the revenues generated by canal dues, Panama has today established itself as a financial centre for Latin America, in part by offering the enticement of banking secrecy. It was one of the first "flag of convenience" nations, and attracts many shipowners to register their vessels in Panama by charging low fees. It remains the world's largest registry, with more than 14,000 merchant ships nominally "Panamanian".

Of today's varied population of 3 million, more than half live within 10 km (6 miles) of the Canal. In the formerly US-controlled Canal Zone, Balboa stands at the Pacific end and Cristóbal on the Caribbean. Adjoining them are the larger, more chaotic and much untidier cities: the capital, Panama City, and Colón, a free-wheeling port next to Cristóbal. The western part of the country is sparsely populated.

With 940 species of birds, 1500 kinds of butterfly, hundreds of rare and exotic plants and animals, Panama foresees a great future in eco-tourism, following the example of Costa Rica.

A BRIEF HISTORY

16th century

The Spanish explorer Rodrigo de Bastidas discovers Panama in 1501. In 1510, Nombre de Dios is founded at the mouth of the River Chagres. Vasco Núñez de Balboa becomes governor of the first permanent settlement; he learns from the local Indians of "a great sea to the South", and with their help he sights the Pacific Ocean in 1513. Panama City is founded on the Pacific coast in 1519 and becomes a base for more expeditions including Pizarro's conquest of Peru. The Camino Real (Royal Road) is opened, linking Panama City with Portobelo on the Caribbean. This route becomes vital in the shipment of treasure from Peru to Spain. Panama is incorporated into the Viceroyalty of Peru in 1542. Sir Francis Drake leads a series of raids on the area, and the Spanish counter by building a comprehensive system of fortifications.

17th century

In 1671 the pirate Henry Morgan attacks the Caribbean coast, taking the fort of San Lorenzo and penetrating all the way to Panama City. He burns the town to the ground and leaves with 200 mules loaded with booty. The settlement is rebuilt two years later on a more easily defensible site.

18th century

Panama is joined to the Viceroyalty of Granada (present-day Colombia) in 1717. Admiral Sir Edward Vernon captures Portobelo in 1739, and San Lorenzo the following year. The Camino Real falls into disuse. Shipping begins to take the Cape Horn route and Panama is half-forgotten.

19th century

In 1821, Panama declares independence from Spain, but soon joins in a union with Colombia. During the gold rush of 1849, hordes of would-be prospectors travel from the east coast of the United States to the west by way of Panama. In 1855 a railway is constructed from Colón to Panama City, facilitating the journey across the isthmus. During the second half of the century, revolution breaks out some 50 times, but Panama remains tied to Colombia. A French company begins excavation of a canal in 1882, under the direction of Ferdinand de Lesseps, builder of the Suez Canal. However, they are forced to give up after seven years of technical and financial problems, and outbreaks of malaria and yellow fever that result in the deaths of 22,000 workers. The United States government tries to acquire the rights, but Colombia does not agree.

20th century–present

The US supports Panama's successful bid for independence in 1903. In exchange, the Canal Zone—a strip of land extending 8 km (5 miles) to either side of the canal—is granted to the US in perpetuity. The area is cleared of disease-carrying mosquitoes and work on the canal goes forward, reaching completion in 1914. In time Panama rejects the perpetual right of the US to the Canal Zone and seeks greater control over the operation of the canal. A new Canal Treaty is ratified in 1977, setting a timetable for the return of the canal to the Republic. The Canal Zone is transferred to Panama on October 1, 1979. Panamanian army officers increasingly interfere in politics; in May 1989 General Manuel Noriega seizes power. US forces invade Panama in December of that year in Operation "Just Cause", deposing Noriega, and detaining him on drugs charges. He is later convicted in Florida and sentenced to 40 years imprisonment. A period of increasing Panamanian participation precedes the final hand-over of the Canal on December 31, 1999. Miraya Moscoso, its first woman president, represents Panama at the ceremonies. In 2004, Martín Torrijos is elected as her successor.

Canal de Panamá

Sightseeing

Panama City

Begin your visit with **Casco Viejo**, the fortified city founded in 1673 to replace Panamá Viejo (Old Panama) after it was destroyed by the pirate Henry Morgan. A few traces remain of the French presence, and there are some interesting churches.

San Felipe is the shabby old quarter towards the end of the rocky peninsula chosen as the site for the refoundation. Here are all the features typical of old Latin American towns: cobblestoned streets, pastel facades, iron grilles over the windows, high-walled convents and mansions. In the tranquil Plaza de Francia stands an obelisk topped by a Gallic cockerel in honour of the French attempt to build a canal. Not far away is **Paseo de las Bóvedas**, a promenade on part of the old city wall.

The nearby **Church of Santo Domingo** has fallen to ruins but its brick and mortar "flat arch", constructed without internal supports, has withstood the test of time. In fact, the evidence of its survival is said to have been a factor in the selection of Panama as the site for the canal, rather than earthquake-prone Costa Rica or Nicaragua. Take time to visit the Museo de Arte Religioso in one of the chapels.

Going up Calle 3, next to the church of San Francisco, you will see the superbly restored **National Theatre**, inaugurated in 1908 by Sarah Bernhardt. By the sea, the **Palacio Presidencial** (President's Palace) occupies a luxurious residence dating from 1673. In the heart of the district, **Plaza de la Independencia**, in front of the 18th-centuy cathedral, is lined with some of the most important buildings of the area. If you are interested in the history of the canal, do not miss the **Museo del Canal Interoceánico** located in the former headquarters of Ferdinand de Lesseps. On Avenida A, the **Church of San José** houses the magnificent Baroque "golden altar", saved from Morgan's raid on the old city, when nuns managed to hide it by covering it in mud.

To the east of Casco Viejo, **Avenida Central**, part-pedestrianized, is the main commercial artery, leading to the business and residential districts of modern Panama City. South of Plaza 5 de Mayo is the **Museo Antropológico Reina Torres de Araúz**. Avenida Central becomes Via España at **El Congrejo**, the residential and commercial district of town. Most of the 80 banks of Panama are located here, in the glass and steel skyscrapers, surrounded by hotels, casinos and condominiums.

Further out, about 7 km (4 miles) from the present city centre, are the ruins of **Panamá Viejo**. Founded on a vulnerable site in 1519, the city was sacked and burned to the ground by the pirate Henry Morgan in 1671. The remains of the cathedral, the original church of San José, Convent of La Merced and various government buildings and barracks can still be seen, as well as King's Bridge, starting point of the Royal Road across the isthmus.

On higher ground only 15 minutes' drive from the centre, the **Metropolitan Nature Park** encompasses 265 ha, mostly tropical rainforest, a green island amid the skyscrapers and traffic. Over 200 species of birds, many lizards and other reptiles, monkeys and other mammals can be spotted from its footpaths. The US Smithsonian Institution operates a research station, with a crane to allow study of the forest canopy.

Balboa

The Panama Canal Commission has its headquarters in the Pacific port of Balboa, which reverted to the Republic of Panama with the abolition of the Canal Zone in 1979. Between the entrance to the Canal and Ancón Hill, Balboa remains a thoroughly American creation, neat, suburban, well-regulated, although the hubbub of Panama City lies only ten minutes away by car. The palm-lined Prado leads from the centre of

THE BIG DITCH

The Panama Canal has operated without a hitch since 1914. A miracle of early 20th-century engineering, the multi-lock canal runs northwest to southeast across the mountainous isthmus of Panama. It extends for a distance of more than 80 km (50 miles), linking the Atlantic and Pacific oceans and reducing the long journey around Cape Horn to a mere 10 hours — instead of weeks or months.

The first ship passed through the new canal on August 15, 1914, marking the culmination of a legendary feat, although the construction of the canal cost dearly: a total of US$ 387 million was spent and many lives were lost to malaria, yellow fever and other tropical diseases. The feasibility of an inter-oceanic canal was debated from the day in 1513 when Balboa first sighted the Pacific. Charles V of Spain, Simón Bolívar and the governments of the United States and Great Britain all gave thought to the problems involved. But it was a French company that first sought permission from Colombia to undertake the task.

Ferdinand de Lesseps, builder of the Suez Canal and by this time 76 years old, made initial surveys in 1881. He proposed a sea-level channel, despite the need for wholesale blasting of the mountainous terrain. Digging began, only to be brought to a halt after 28 km (18 miles) by financial problems, inadequate machinery and the high death toll. De Lesseps was prosecuted by the French government and sentenced to five years imprisonment, but this harsh verdict was overturned on appeal.

The United States government opened negotiations with Colombia for the rights and property secured by the French, but failed to come to an agreement. In 1903 Panama declared independence, ceding the Canal Zone to the US in perpetuity.

US army engineers headed by George Washington Goethals rejected the sea-level plan in favour of a design incorporating a series of locks to raise and lower ships in transit. Each lock was provided with twin chambers to allow ships to move in opposite directions at the same time.

Ships have become so big in recent years that they have outgrown the canal. A wider waterway is under construction, due for completion in 2015.

Balboa to the Canal Administration Building in **Balboa Heights**. Inside the rotunda are four murals by New Yorker William Van Ingen illustrating the labour involved in building the Canal. Statues honour US president Theodore Roosevelt and Ferdinand de Lesseps, and at the far end of the Prado a marble monument commemorates George Washington Goethals, the American colonel who masterminded the construction.

A long peninsula juts into the Pacific south of Balboa. It is the site of **Fuerte Amador**, former headquarters of the Panamanian Defence Force, held by US forces from 1989 to 1994. It has been converted into a modern marina and resort, with an attractive shopping plaza. A causeway links the peninsula to the fortified islands of Naos, Perico and Flamenco and their beaches.

Isla Taboga

From Balboa, regular ferry boats make the hour's journey to Taboga, 19 km (12 miles) to the south. Known as the Isle of Flowers, it was settled as early as 1515; the tiny white church on the main square is said to be the second-oldest in the Americas. Little has changed, calm still reigns and there is no traffic apart from the bicycles that you can rent to ride along forest paths through the hilly interior. The air is fragrant with jasmine and hibiscus. Visitors today are drawn by the beaches, clear blue sea and water sports: snorkelling, scuba-diving, water-skiing, windsurfing and fishing. On the north coast, 100,000 pelicans nest in April and May.

The Canal and its Locks

The Panama Canal traverses a landscape of remarkable beauty. Throughout the transit the panorama is ever-changing, and the intricate workings of the locks are fascinating.

After receiving permission to begin the crossing, ships pass beneath the impressive steel arch of the **Puente de las Américas** (Americas Bridge), more than 1,653 m (5,425 ft) long. Set high above the narrow ribbon of the canal, the bridge spans the entrance to the Pacific and forms an important link in the Inter-American Highway. They head for the **Miraflores Locks**. The gates here are higher than those at the Atlantic end of the canal, owing to the greater variation in Pacific tides. Although there isn't much room to spare—the twin chambers in each lift measure 33.5 by 306 m (110 by 1,000 ft)—ships pass neatly through the three sets of lifts, helped along by powerful mechanical "mules" mounted on special tracks. In days gone by, real animals did this work. A platform enables visitors to watch the ships rising to reach the level of Miraflores Lake (9 a.m–5 p.m.); there is also a visitor centre showing a film and scale models.

The captain of a vessel does not do the navigating; pilots familiar with the locks take complete control. Technicians in the control tower between the lifts open and close the gates to each lift and regulate the flow of water. Smaller vessels may go through in pairs, yoked together, especially yachts which would otherwise be thrown around by the swirling water during the filling of the lock.

At **Pedro Miguel Locks**, a lift raises ships 9.5 m (31 ft) from Miraflores Lake. Still guided by a tug, they then enter the **Gaillard Cut**, site of the continental divide. This spectacular passage between sheer cliffs is just wide enough for two-way traffic, except in the case of very large ships. It has been widened from its original 91.5 m (300 ft) along its entire length to a minimum of 152 m (498 ft); this work was completed in 1970. The cut was originally opened in a seven-year-long blasting operation supervised by David Gaillard of the US Army Corps of Engineers. A good part of the 273,000 tonnes of dynamite used in the canal's construction was detonated here. Off to one side, opposite Gold Hill, lies Contractor's Hill, lowered about 12 m (40 ft) in 1954 when landslides threatened.

After 13 km (8 miles), the Gaillard Cut opens into **Gatún Lake**, an immense artificial reservoir of 418 sq km (163 sq miles), created by the construction of a dam on the Chagres River. The lake supplies the water for the locks—around 197 million litres (43 million gallons) per transit. In contrast to the sophisticated workings of the locks, the virgin jungle all around, its creeping vines and exotic vegetation providing an extraordinary counterpoint to the concrete and steel of the canal itself.

When the lake was formed in 1914, animals in the area re-

Canal Figures

Every year some 13,000–14,000 ships pass through the "Big Ditch", each bringing the Panama Canal Company an average of about US$ 54,000. A 100,000 tonne cruise ship might pay over $150,000. (However expensive it may seem, the toll is a bargain, as the Cape Horn journey would cost far more.) The smallest sum ever paid is 36 cents, charged to Richard Halliburton in 1928 after he swam from one end of the canal to the other. The toll is calculated mainly by weight!

treated to the high ground of what has become **Barro Colorado Island**, now a nature reserve. It can be visited by prior arrangement with the Smithsonian Institute at Ancón.

After crossing the lake, the ships reach the **Gatún Locks** (8 a.m. –4 p.m.) where they descend a total of 26 m (85 ft) to sea level. The last section of the journey leads to the port of Cristóbal, through a channel cut through the mangrove. From ocean to ocean, the change in level is imperceptible, the Atlantic is only 18 cm (7 inches) lower than the Pacific.

The Canal Area

Past the Miraflores Locks, 20 km (12 miles) north of Balboa, the **Jardín Botánico Summit** was created in 1923 by the canal administration. The pathways run through a zoo and a park planted with thousands of plants. The Sendero El Charco is the most easily accessible of the paths entering the **Soberanía National Park**, a stretch of forest between Gatún and Alajuela lakes.

To the east, the big **Chagres National Park** includes the river of the same name, the main source of water for the canal, providing 80 per cent of its needs. You can observe iguanas, monkeys and toucans in the humid tropical forest, and there are opportunities for rafting.

At the Atlantic entrance to the canal, **Colón** is a major shopping centre and bustling city with a population of some 75,000. Front Street, lined with various duty-free shops, has seen better days, but the Free Zone to the east is a booming centre for the transshipment of bulk goods. Individuals, however, can also make purchases here. Apart from the cathedral, the beach and a scattering of monuments, Colón has little in the way of tourist sights. This is rather a city of nocturnal pleasures and rough bars, patronized mainly by sailors. Don't walk alone, and keep a tight hold of your possessions. (Better still, don't carry any.) On the other side of the railway line is **Cristóbal**, a busy port.

High on a promontory on the west bank of the canal, at the mouth of the Chagres River, **Fort San Lorenzo** was one of the main Spanish defences of the New World. It resisted 11 days before falling into the hands of Morgan and his 1200 men. It has been superbly restored.

Now no more than a village and quiet anchorage 44 km (27 miles east of Colón, **Portobelo** was in the 16th and early 17th centuries the most important port and market in the New World. Every year, a great fair was held to mark the arrival of a fleet of galleons from Spain, laden with luxury

MOLAS

The best-known products of the San Blas islands are the colourful *mola* needlework panels made and worn by the Cuna women. The word refers to a blouse, and the panels, usually about 46 cm (18 in) across and 30 cm (18 in) high, are sewn on to the fronts and sometimes the backs of their blouses. But their popularity with visitors means that they now come in all shapes and sizes, as mats, pictures and other souvenirs. Some are crude and gaudy, but fine stitching and subtler colours can still be found.

The technique, sometimes called reverse appliqué, involves sewing several layers of different fabrics together, cutting down through them in a pattern—simple or complex—something like a contour map, turning the cut edges under and sewing them down with tiny stitches. Early designs were mainly abstract or geometric, and symmetrical, with fine lines. Then birds, animals and snakes became popular, especially showing smaller, perhaps foetal, animals or birds inside. Now almost anything goes: planes, ships, cigarette packets, copies of commercial logos or advertisements. How did the fashion begin? The generally accepted theory is that the Cuna formerly wore very little clothing (sensibly in this climate) but painted and tattooed their bodies with elaborate designs. When missionaries arrived and taught them to cover up, they adapted the designs to fabric.

products and manufactured goods. In more than fair exchange, they took on a precious cargo of gold and silver which had been brought across the isthmus of Panama by the Royal Road and stored in the warehouses of Portobelo, strongly fortified against pirate attack. Their ruins can still be seen, as well as the Church of San Felipe, home of the Black Christ of Portobelo, a famous image credited with saving the town from a cholera epidemic. When the Royal Road fell into disuse, the world forgot Portobelo.

A track leads to the pier where boats leave for **Isla Grande**, populated by a few hundred fisherfolk descended from African slaves, has idyllic beaches and coconut plantations.

San Blas Islands

There are said to be 365 islands and islets in this archipelago off the north coast about 120 km (75 miles) east of Colón, and half-an-hour by air from Panama City. Scattered in the turquoise sea, most are mere sand-bars, and deserted, but about 50 of them, dotted with thatched huts, are home to around 45,000 Cuna (or Kuna) Indian people. Finding refuge here in the 19th century after being driven from their land on the isthmus, they have fiercely defended their autonomy, language and traditions. Following a revolt in 1925, they regained a foothold on the mainland, a coastal strip to allow them to grow some crops. Coconuts are still a mainstay and source of income. The men fish and work the fields, but this is essentially a matriarchal society and women run the ruling council. After marriage, a man moves into his wife's household, and girl babies are welcomed with far greater enthusiasm than boys. Women wear elaborate traditional dress: mola blouses, skirts made of colourful printed fabrics, scarves, pearls, jewelled combs and anklets and gold rings through their noses.

Only a few of the islands welcome tourists: Tigre, Wichubwala and Nalunega; cruise ships call in at Cartí.

Darién

At the eastern extremity of Panama, the Darién rainforest, jungle and swamps form a natural barrier separating Central and South America. Many of the region's Chocó Indian people count this as a blessing. In spite of the lack of roads, they have already been the victims of attacks by landless peasants and cattle herders who covet this green wilderness and would slash and burn its forests. The heart of Darién, the National Park desig-

A far cry from the bustle of big ships in the canal, a native boat in San Blas Islands.

nated in 1983 along the border with Colombia and the Pacific coast, cut by deep river valleys, is the home of an astonishing range of wildlife; caimans, tapirs, ocelots and hundreds of species of birds, including vividly coloured macaws.

The West
Fine beaches begin close to the Pacific entrance to the Canal, and stretch right round the Gulf of Panama from **Punta Chame** to **Farallón**. The pleasant hill station of **El Valle** is known for its Sunday market, where local Indian people sell their craft work—ceramics, wood and soapstone carvings and basketry—as well as vegetables, fruit and lovely orchids. The surrounding hills are great for hiking and horseback riding. In the Altos de Campana park, you may see the famous golden frogs of Panama, and remarkable trees with square trunks.

Extending 100 km (62 miles) into the Pacific, the broad **Azuero Peninsula** was colonized in the 16th century and preserves many colonial buildings and folk traditions. Carnival is celebrated with special enthusiasm. **Chitré** on the eastern side is a good starting point, with its fine cathedral and history museum. Nearby in **Los Santos**, the house where Panamanian independence was declared is now the Museum of Nationality, and at **Guararé**, the Manuel Zárate Museum celebrates the costumes, customs and crafts of the region. Las Tablas has a beautiful colonial church as well as claiming to be the home of the *pollera*, the robe which is now the national dress. All along the coast as far as Pedasi are magnificent, usually deserted beaches. **Isla Iguana** is a nature reserve for the big lizards, and for many sea birds.

Chiriquí means "valley of the moon" in the language of the local Guaymí Indians; it's a term of praise for the cool, green highlands and mountain streams of Panama's westernmost province. **David** is the agreeable provincial capital, a centre of cattle ranching with a famous rodeo, but vacationers head inland to the mountain town of **Boquete**, for troutfishing, river-rafting, mountain climbing and a dip in the hot springs. Only 20 km (12 miles) west of Boquete is **Mount Barú**, 3475 m (11,398 ft), a live volcano with six craters although currently dormant. From the summit, it's possible on clear days to see both the Caribbean and the Pacific. On the lower slopes, the fertile volcanic soil and cool climate is ideal for growing coffee and flowers.

The northwest corner of Panama is more a part of the Caribbean than the Latin American world. Facing the expanse of the Chiriquí Lagoon, discovered by Columbus in 1502, are around 300 coral islands and islets, **Bocas del Toro** fringed by banana plantations, coconut palms and sandy shores. The people are descended from African slaves brought to work the former sugar estates. English with a Caribbean lilt is the main language, and the older houses have a Georgian look. **Bastimentos National Park**, embracing many of the islands, offers some of the best snorkelling and diving in Panama, with 200 species of tropical fish, manatees and turtles which come ashore to lay eggs.

Dining Out

Panama's polyglot population brings all its diversity to the local culinary scene. *Sancocho*, the national dish, combines chicken, yucca, sweet corn, plantain, potatoes, onions and coriander in a rich stew. *Ropa vieja* contains beef, garlic, fried onions, tomatoes and green peppers. The fresh seafood is excellent—shrimp, clams, oysters, rock lobster and octopus—and the fishing fleet brings in a good selection. The Cuna Indians prepare fish dishes with rice, yucca, plantain bananas and spices all stewed in coconut milk.

Sopa de gloria—sponge cake soaked in cream and rum—will satisfy just about any sweet tooth. Other popular desserts are *arroz con cacao*, chocolate-rice pudding, and *guanabana* (sweet soursop) ice cream. Fresh tropical and other fruits are a healthy alternative.

Drinks

Beer and mineral water are readily obtainable, as well as fruit juices, every known variety of liquor including local cane spirit, and a choice of imported wines.

Shopping

Panama's renown as a shopping mecca is widespread. A first priority for many is the wide range of low-duty or duty-free luxury goods. Popular, too, is the array of Oriental and Indian fabrics, clothing and other articles. But the most unusual items are the handicrafts from Panama itself: *bateas*, wooden trays; *chaquiras*, beadwork necklaces; mahogany bowls; soapstone carvings from El Valle; and *molas*, multi-coloured cloth panels made by the Cuna Indians, normally used for the fronts of blouses. Some of the most sought-after are those that have faded from their original brightness, having been worn and washed, presumably because their makers especially liked them and kept them for a while before selling them.

PRACTICAL INFORMATION

Banks. Open Monday to Friday 8 a.m.–1.30 p.m., Saturday 8 a.m.– noon.

Climate. Tropical, with high humidity (around 90 per cent) and high temperatures, reaching 30-34°C (86–91°F) or more at any time of year on the coast. The nights are mercifully cooler, and so are the mountain areas in the west of the country. The so-called summer *(verano)* corresponds to the dry season, beginning around January and lasting until April. Winter *(invierno)* is just as hot and lasts from May to November; this is when most of the rain falls. The Pacific coast is sunny almost all year round, while the Caribbean (northern) coast is wetter. The country is outside the usual hurricane zone.

Clothing. Lightweight washable cottons are recommended, with a wrap or jacket for fierce air-conditioning. An umbrella is useful in the wet months.

Currency. The *balboa* (B or PAB), equivalent to the US dollar, is divided into 100 centésimos. There is no local paper currency; US dollars are used. US coins are also interchangeable with local coins of the same size and value: penny (1 ¢), nickel (5 ¢), dime (10 ¢), quarter (25 ¢) and half-dollar (50 ¢), the last being less used.

Electricity. Generally 110 or 120 volts AC, 60 Hz. Plugs are of the American type, with two flat prongs, or two flat and one round.

Safety. In towns, particularly in Colón and Panama City, take reasonable precautions. Do not wear jewellery or carry valuables or large amounts of money on you. Avoid walking alone, especially at night.

Shops. Monday toSaturday 8 or 9 a.m.–7 p.m., Sunday 10 a.m.–7 p.m.

Time. GMT –5 all year round.

Tipping. The gratuity is left to the discretion of the client. In restaurants about 10 per cent is appropriate, but if you dine in an establishment frequented by American tourists, your waiter will probably expect a tip of 15 to 20 per cent. Taxi drivers are not generally tipped: agree the fare in advance.

Water. Tap water is safe to drink in Cristóbal, Balboa and Panama City, but bottled mineral water tastes better.

THE HARD FACTS

To help you plan your trip, here are some of the practical details you should know about Central America.

Airports

On the whole, the international airports have the most basic facilities and services, though you can generally hire a car, obtain tourist information and change money. The banks keep normal opening hours, and are almost always closed on Sunday, sometimes on Saturday, and at lunchtime. Keep your eye on the departure board as sometimes the domestic flights leave early (particularly in the Honduras).

International flights for **Belize** land at the Philip S. W. Goldson airport (BZE), 16 km (10 miles) northwest of Belize City. The airport bus takes 30 min to the city centre. Taxis are available; agree on the price in advance. The airport has duty-free shops, bank, shops, restaurant and bar. Belmopan is 84 km (52 miles) from Belize City. There are scheduled flights daily to each of the main towns.

Costa Rica's main airport, Juan Santamaría (SJO), is 15 km (9 miles) northwest of the capital, San José, near the town of Alajuela. You will find restaurants, duty-free shops, exchange offices, cash-distributors, car-hire counters and a small tourist office. To get to San José by taxi, you must pay at the cash-desk before joining the queue. The country's second international airport, Daniel Oduber Quirós, is 13 km (8 miles) west of Liberia, in Guanacaste province. It is served by several American airlines and offers a good alternative port of entry for people heading for the north Pacific coast. It has, however, fewer services and you have to take a taxi to the car-hire offices.

The international airport of **El Salvador** is San Salvador (SAL), 62 km (38 miles) from the city. Coaches operate every 30 minutes and take 40 minutes to reach the centre. Taxis are available. Duty-free shops, restaurant, car hire, pharmacy, bank, bureau de change, tourist information. Domestic flights to San Miguel, La Unión and Usulután.

In **Guatemala**, the international airport of La Aurora (GUA) is located 6 km (4 miles) south of the Guatemala City. A bus runs to the city but it's better to take a taxi (20 minutes travel time). Duty-free shop, car hire, bar, buffet, restaurant, post office, bank, bureau de change, tourist information. There are daily flights to El Petén and several towns.

The main airport for **Honduras** is Tegucigalpa (TGU) at Toncontin, 5 km (3 miles) southeast of the city. Taxis and buses are available to the centre. Airport facilities include duty-free shop, bar, restaurant, bank, post office, first aid, and car hire. Other international airports are La Mesa for San Pedro Sula (SAP), Golosón for La Ceiba (LCE) and Dr Juan Manuel Galvez for Roatán (RTB). Daily services link Tegucigalpa with the other main towns, and there are also flights to the Bay Islands.

Flights for **Nicaragua** land at Managua International Airport (MGA), 12 km (7 miles) north of the city. Bus and taxi services run to the city; travel time is 15 minutes. Duty-free shop, bars, restaurants, bank, post office, pharmacy, tourist information, car hire. Domestic flights serve many cities but have been classed as Category 2 as they do not comply with international safety standards.

The main airport in **Panama** is Panama City (PTY), Tocumén, 27 km (17 miles) northeast of the city. Travel time by bus or taxi is 30-60 minutes. Duty-free shop, restaurant, bank, chemist, car hire. Domestic airlines operate out of Aeropuerto Marcos A. Gelabert, located in the Albrook area of Panama City.

Bargaining

The general custom in the markets is to bargain for everything you buy, especially souvenirs. The technique is to offer between half and three-quarters the amount the stallholder proposes, and gradually you move together towards an agreement. If the seller thinks your offer is too low in proportion to the amount of work involved, it will probably be refused. But particularly in poverty-stricken regions, some people will accept a very low price out of necessity. What you decide is a matter of your own conscience.

Climate

There are two seasons. Summer *(verano),* which corresponds to the dry season, starts beween November and January and lasts until April. Summer is shorter, the closer you are to the south. It is the best time of year to visit Central America: the humidity and temperatures are more bearable. Winter *(invierno)* is warm. It lasts from May to October and is marked by rainfall. Local figures vary enormously: if the Pacific coast is sunny most of the year, the Caribbean shores, swept by the tradewinds, are much more humid (with local variations). Because of the altitude, the rainy season can be quite unpleasant on the high plateaux: it is cold, especially in Guatemala, and the volcanoes are covered by cloud all day long. The rain, alternating with violent storms, falls mostly in late afternoon and during the night, but the mornings are generally dry. Temperatures vary between a maximum of 30–35°C on the coast and a minimum of 10–12°C on the high plateaux. Sometimes it can freeze at high altitudes. All year round, the sea varies from 25 to 29°C.

Hurricanes (winds above 120 kph, accompanied by torrential rain and huge waves) can occur between June and November. Advanced tracking systems give plenty of warning. Radar, hurricane, hunter flights, satellite pictures and forecasts combine to produce a hurricane watch, which goes into effect 24 hours before a major storm is expected.

Clothing

Take loose-fitting, comfortable clothes, preferably in cotton. People dress casually, but not carelessly: Central America is largely conservative and catholic, and revealing clothes are frowned upon. Don't forget your bathing costume, but keep it for the beach and the swimming pool. You will need a sun hat wherever you go. The local people often shade themselves with an umbrella.

Don't forget to pack a few warm clothes, jackets or sweaters for the cool evenings of the high plateaux; you will also need something waterproof to protect you from the tropical rains. On forest walks, wear thick, long trousers even if you are too hot, otherwise you risk being stung by plants, not to mention the hordes of biting insects. High boots are indispensable, in case you encounter a snake or a trapdoor spider. If you are going to the Caribbean coast, take plastic shoes to avoid coral cuts. In any case, try to avoid walking on the coral as it is very fragile.

Communications

International direct dialling is available in all Central American countries. The most convenient way to use public phones is with a pre-paid telephone card, *tarjeta telefonica*. For mobile phones, roaming is available in many areas; check with your company before leaving home. There are Internet cafés in all the main towns.

Mail for Europe can take anything from one to three weeks.

Private courier services are available but of course much more expensive.

Driving

Cars can be hired in the international airports of all the Central American capitals, as well as in the ports of entry and the larger towns. It's best (and cheaper) to book ahead through a reliable international company. A four-wheel drive vehicle can be useful, especially during the rainy season—and all year round in Belize or Costa Rica. The minimum age requirement is generally 25, sometimes 21. A national driving licence is recognized by the hire companies, but just in case, you should also have an international licence. Make sure you are fully insured, especially against theft.

On the whole, the Panamerican and the major highways of the Central American road network are of satisfactory quality. Belize, Nicaragua and Costa Rica are the least favoured in this respect. Whatever the country, there are many tracks and often these are the only means of access. Signposting is excellent in Costa Rica and Honduras, and often totally absent in Panama and Guatemala, where you will often have to ask your way. You will need a good road map: if possible buy it before leaving home as they are hard to find on the spot.

The highway code is scrupulously respected in Costa Rica, where there are numerous fines for all kinds of contraventions, including bad parking. The other countries are more lax. Local drivers tend to get over-excited and pull out unexpectedly or overtake inadvertently. Stay calm, and all will be well. Speed limits vary from one country to the other. Generally, the maximum authorized speed is 80 or 90 kph on major highways (there are very few motorways). Try to avoid driving at night: many of the buses and some cars drive without headlights, or simply don't have any. Note that in the capital cities, and more particularly in Panama City, directions are reversed on some roads at rush hour. One-way roads are badly indicated, or not indicated at all.

Electricity

Mainly 110 volts, 60 Hz, but 220 volts are increasingly used in Honduras. Plugs are of the American type, with two flat pins, or two flat and one round. Power cuts are fairly frequent. Take an adapter and transformer for your electrical appliances.

Formalities

Check with your travel agent or the consulate of the countries you will be visiting for the latest information about the documents you will need: regulations are different according to nationality and frequently subject to change.

A passport valid for 6 months after your return date is sufficient for entry into most of the Central American countries. Some airlines ask you to prove you have a return or continuing ticket before letting you board the plane.

Personal effects (cameras, binoculars, sporting equipment, etc) are exempt of customs tax. It can be useful to carry customs clearance forms (or proof of purchase) for your equipment. It is forbidden to export pre-Columbian artefacts without a special authorization.

Health

No vaccinations are required for Central America, but make sure your boosters are up to date. Vaccinations against typhoid and hepatitis are advised, especially if you are visiting the coastal regions, and an anti-malarial treatment if you are going to the Caribbean or Pacific coasts. Your doctor will advise you.

The biggest health problems are caused by the sun, mosquitoes, water and food. Take all the necessary precautions against sunburn and sunstroke, especially the first days, using a high-factor sun cream, a sunhat and a T-shirt. The tropical sun is much stronger than you imagine—four to five times more intense than in Europe. You will need a good insect repellent to keep the mosquitoes away, as well as a net to sleep under. Stick to bottled mineral water, avoid raw vegetables, unpeeled fruit, ice cream, ice cubes and under-cooked meat. On the coast, beware of coral cuts, which can easily get infected if they are not treated properly.

Health care varies from one country to another, from excellent in Costa Rica to mediocre in Nicaragua. The main problem in the poor countries is the lack of medication. Take a basic first aid kit with you, containing aspirin or another pain-killer, an anti-diarrhoea drug, disinfectant, bandages, a cream to soothe burns, etc. If you are taking prescribed medicines, make sure you have all you will need. Make sure your health insurance covers repatriation in case of severe illness.

Holidays and Festivals

The perfect excuse for the people to let off steam, numerous festivals are held during the year. They are celebrated with enthusiasm and even excess, notably as regards the consumption of alcohol. However, they are invariably exceptional occasions, bearing witness to the strength of religious beliefs and national fervour.

The most important event of the year is Easter: all the accommodation is booked up months in advance. It is impossible to drive around, to find a room or a shop open.

The following holidays are celebrated in every Central American country:

January 1	*New Year's Day*
March-April	*Easter*
May 1	*Labour Day*
September 15	*Independence Day* (except in Belize)
October 12	*Discovery of America*
December 25	*Christmas Day*

The following holidays are specific to each country.

Belize

March 9	*Baron Bliss Day*
April 21	*Queen's Birthday*
May 24	*Commonwealth Day*
September 10	*St George's Caye Day*
September 21	*Independence Day*
November 19	*Garífuna Settlement Day*

Costa Rica

March 19	*St Joseph's Day*
April 11	*Juan Santamaria Day (Battle of Rivas)*
June 29	*St Peter and St Paul's Day*
July 25	*Guanacaste Day*
August 2	*Virgin of Los Angeles Day*
August 15	*Assumption, Mother's Day*
December 8	*Immaculate Conception*

El Salvador

May 13	*Pilgrimage of the Virgin of Fátima* (at Cojutepeque)
Early August	*Corpus Christi*
November 2	*All Saints*
November 5	*Anniversary of the Call for Independence*

Guatemala

Easter	*Holy Week* (Antigua)
August 15	*Assumption* (Nebaj, Sololá)
October 20	*Anniversary of the Revolution*
November 1	*All Saints* (Todos Santos Cuchumatán)

Every village celebrates its patron saint once a year. It is a unique occasion to discover Indian traditions. The most interesting is the Feast of St Thomas, December 21 at Chichicastenango.

Honduras

February 3	*Fiesta of the Virgin of Suyapa*
April 14	*Americas Day*

End May	*Carnival of La Ceiba*
October 3	*Francisco Morazán Day*
October 21	*Armed Forces Day*

Nicaragua

July 19	*Liberation Day*
September 14	*Battle of San Jacinto*
November 2	*All Souls Day*
December 7–8	*Immaculate Conception*

Panamá

January 9	*Martyrs' Day*
February	*Carnival of Panama City*
Easter	*Holy Week* (at Villa de Los Santos, Azuero Peninsula)
August 15	*Panama City Day*
November 1–4	*All Saints* and *Independence Day*
November 10	*First Cry for Independence*
November 28	*Independence conceded by Spain*
December 8:	*Mothers' Day*

Language

Apart from in Belize and the Caribbean coast of certain countries, Spanish is the main language of Central America. English is spoken by the black populations—whose ancestors were slaves, deported or refugees from the British colonies—and by all those who have links with the tourism industry. Many Indian languages of the Maya group are still spoken in Guatemala (Quiché, Cakchiquel, Mam…) and others in Panama, in the San Blas islands. In most Hispanic countries, it is possible to follow Spanish language courses, generally including lodgings with a family. This is a speciality of Antigua in Guatemala, but you can also study Spanish in Salvador or Honduras.

Money

Whatever the country and local currency, the US dollar is welcome everywhere. So as well as your credit card, take cash and travellers cheques in dollars (if they are in small denominations you can sometimes use travellers cheques instead of cash). It's also a good idea to ask for small notes when you exchange money, as large notes might be refused in shops and restaurants.

Photography

If you are still using standard film, take sufficient supplies with you, as it is expensive in Central America, and probably stored in hot and humid conditions. If you do buy film in airport boutiques or souvenir shops, check the sell-by date. For your digital camera, it might be useful to take an extra memory card as they fill up more quickly than you think!

Do not take pictures of "strate-gic" buildings such as army barracks, airports, police stations, and so on. And don't forget to protect your material from the sun, dust and humidity. The light is extremely intense during the hot hours of the day; a lens hood will come in useful.

Safety

On the whole, the Central American countries are safe for tourists. In the capitals, as in the rest of the world, you need to take the usual precautions against pickpockets and petty thieves: do not carry large sums of money, don't wear flashy jewellery and leave your extra cash and travel documents in the hotel safe. Make several photocopies of your passport, driving licence, plane tickets, etc., and keep them in separate places, with a copy on your person. You can also scan them and upload them as an e-mail attachment sent to yourself, so you can always access them in case of loss or theft.

From Belize to Panama, the Caribbean coast is infamous for muggings, especially in areas frequented by tourists: avoid wandering around at night (or take a taxi) and keep a few dollars in your pocket ready to hand over. Colón and Panama City are reputedly dangerous. Some isolated regions such as the north of Nicaragua and the volcanoes in Guatemala still have gangs of bandits, and there are still minefields in the central and northern regions of Nicaragua. But generally the political situation in all the Central American countries except Guatemala is considered stable, and usually, travel is uneventful.

Before leaving home, you can obtain up-to-date advice from the website of your ministry for foreign affairs, such as:

UK: www.fco.gov.uk
USA: travel.state.gov
Canada: www.voyage.gc.ca

Sport

From the Caribbean to the Pacific, water sports prevail. Sailboarding, diving in the crystalline waters of the Caribbean (Belize cayes and the Bay islands of Honduras, etc.) and surfing along the Pacific Coast (Costa Rica in particular), everything rhymes with ocean. Deep-sea fishing is also practised in all the Pacific ports, with Panama the top choice.

If you prefer freshwater to salt, you can go kayaking or rafting on the swift-running rivers of Panama, Guatemala and Costa

Rica. You can also play tennis or golf in the big hotels or near the main cities. Trekking is a favourite activity, especially around the principal volcanoes, while horseback riding is ideal for discovering the forests of Costa Rica, the Petén in Guatemala, the beaches and the Maya sites of Honduras: the horse is perfectly adapted to these terrains.

Tipping

The *propina* is left to the discretion of the client. Waiters in popular restaurants will probably not expect anything, whereas those in places frequented by American tourists (Belize cayes, Roatán, Panama, etc.) are used to receiving generous tips equivalent to 15–20% of the bill. A small note is sufficient for porters.

Toilets

You'll find public toilets in the airports, railway stations, bus stations, museums and some service stations. Do not expect too much. If you are fastidious, use hotel toilets, or those in a café, as long as you buy at least a drink.

Transport

Local transport is mainly limited to buses, slow to leave the stops, but shooting along like cannonballs once they are let loose on the road. Depending on the country, the buses are run privately or publicly, but wherever you are, they are likely to be run down. Quite often, they are ancient recycled American school buses. In their carefree second life, they roll along to the songs of Julio Iglesias, under the watchful eye of the Virgin Mary. "Dios me guia" (God is my guide), proclaims a notice above the driver's seat. In Panama, the buses are all gaily painted. It's best not to use public transport at night.

Regular boats run to the Belize cayes and the Bay Islands of Honduras, but elsewhere, service is haphazard. The water taxis in Belize do not always meet international security standards, disregard warnings of bad weather and are overloaded.

General editor
Barbara Ender-Jones

English adaptation
Jack Altman

Design
Karin Palazzolo

Layout
Luc Malherbe
Matias Joliet

Photo credits
istockphoto.com/Dan Wood: p. 1
istockphoto.com/Sebastian Duda: p. 4 (frog)
istockphoto.com/
Roberto A. Sanchez: p. 4 (bananas)
Frumm/hemis.fr: p. 4 (costumes)
Frances/hemis.fr: p. 4 (bus)

Maps
JPM Publications
Elsner & Schichor

Copyright © 2008
JPM Publications S.A.
12, avenue William-Fraisse,
1006 Lausanne, Suisse
information@jpmguides.com
http://www.jpmguides.com/

Every care has been taken to verify the information in the guide, but the publisher cannot accept responsibility for any errors that may have occurred. If you spot an inaccuracy or a serious omission, please let us know.

Printed in Switzerland
11892.00.2396
Weber/Bienne
Edition 2008